Chris
Christophersen

Eugene O'Neill

Chris Christophersen

A Play in Three Acts (Six Scenes)

**Foreword by
Leslie Eric Comens**

Random House · New York

Library of Congress Cataloging in Publication Data

O'Neill, Eugene, 1888–1953.
Chris Christophersen: a play in three acts (six scenes)

The original version of the play which was later rewritten and was presented in 1921 as: Anna Christie.
Reprint of the author's typescript. Originally issued: West Point Pleasant, N.J., c1919. With new foreword.
I. Title.
PS3529.N5C5 1982 812'.52   82-40135
ISBN 0-394-52531-0   AACR2

Foreword

EUGENE O'NEILL wrote prolifically, completing more than sixty plays. Thirty-three of them were written during the short period from the spring of 1913 *(A Wife for a Life)* to the spring of 1919 *(Chris Christophersen)*: twenty-four one-act and nine full-length plays; yet, until the spring of 1919, only eleven of the one-acts were staged and none of the full-lengths. For the maturing O'Neill, serious drama came to require breadth of treatment,[1] and it was of increasing concern to him to have his full-length plays produced. Even as early as 1914, with his first two long plays *Bread and Butter* and *Servitude*, O'Neill wished for productions, submitting his efforts to George C. Tyler, his father's friend and a prominent producer. When John D. Williams optioned *Beyond the Horizon* in April 1918, O'Neill thought that his dream would shortly be realized; when Tyler accepted *Chris Christophersen* and *The Straw* in May 1919 and in September 1919, respectively, O'Neill saw their receptions as further fulfillment. But by the late fall of 1919, O'Neill had become discouraged: Williams had done nothing for a year and a half, and Tyler, who had six months earlier

---

[1] After 1919, as he grew as an artist, O'Neill was to write only two more one-act plays because he began to think in larger and longer terms: *Strange Interlude* (nine acts); *Mourning Becomes Electra* (thirteen acts); *The Iceman Cometh* (4½ hours); the trilogy *Myth Plays for the God-Forsaken*, to include *Dynamo, Days Without End* and *It Cannot Be Mad* (unfinished); the eight-play projected monodramas of *By Way of Obit*, of which only *Hughie* was completed; and the eleven-play cycle *A Tale of Possessors Self-Dispossessed*, of which *A Touch of the Poet, More Stately Mansions* and *The Calms of Capricorn* survive in some form.

promised a fall production for *Chris*, [2] now told O'Neill it would be delayed until 1920. O'Neill then threatened Williams with loss of his option, and Williams decided to stage *Beyond the Horizon* at special matinées rather than lose the property; O'Neill pressured Tyler, and Tyler finally agreed to move forward with the *Chris* production.

Beyond the Horizon opened in New York on February 3, 1920, at a matinée at the Morosco Theatre, and was a critical and popular success. Tyler acted quickly to capitalize on its reception and decided to preview *Chris* in several East Coast cities and then bring it to Broadway. *Chris* opened in Atlantic City, New Jersey, on March 8, 1920, at the Apollo Theatre, with Emmett Corrigan as Chris and Lynn Fontanne, an English protegée of Laurette Taylor, as Anna. On March 15 it moved to the Broad Theatre in Philadelphia for a week, and folded. It never had another performance.

Chris is a strongly autobiographical play, incorporating material from O'Neill's experiences as a seaman, from his days of living at a saloon in Lower Manhattan, and from his relationship with the real Chris Christophersen. [3] As will be seen, O'Neill's representative in the play is Paul Andersen.

The action of *Chris* takes place in 1910 at a saloon in New York, on board a barge at anchor in New York and en route to Boston, and on a steam freighter en route to and at anchor in Buenos Aires. In 1910 O'Neill worked on the clipper ship *Charles Racine* from Boston to Buenos

---

[2] O'Neill and the critics referred to the play by this abbreviated title.

[3] Chris Christophersen was born in Tonsberg, Norway, at the time when Norway was ruled by Sweden. He drowned in New York harbor on October 25, 1917.

Aires; in 1911 he returned as a seaman to New York on the freighter *Ikala*. He conflated these two by making the *Londonderry* in *Chris* a steam freighter en route from Boston to Buenos Aires.

O'Neill's knowledge of transatlantic passenger ships had been gained during the two crossings on which he worked: from New York to Southampton on July 22, 1911 on board the S.S. *New York* and the return voyage on August 9 on board the S.S. *Philadelphia*. Between the Buenos Aires–New York and New York–Southampton voyages, O'Neill discovered a waterfront saloon at 252 Fulton Street in New York known as Jimmy "the Priest's," where he lived for several months in an upstairs room. While there, O'Neill not only met the sailors who were the models for the characters in Act One, Scene 1, but also became close to "Jimmy the Priest" (the Johnny "the Priest" of *Chris*) and to Chris Christophersen. His descriptions of them are not fictionalized.

What O'Neill did fictionalize was the story of Chris. The only biographic information he used was that Chris was a former clipper-ship sailor, now a barge captain, who had been to Buenos Aires, and who referred often to the sea as "dat ole davil."

As the fictional Chris was modeled on the real Chris, so Paul Andersen was modeled on O'Neill. Both were approximately the same age; both had the same physical attributes (except for hair color); both had dropped out of college; both were in love with the sea; both were dreamers; both had, as Andersen explains in Act Three, Scene 2, "swallowed the anchor": Andersen from ambitionless contentment, and O'Neill from ambitionless self-contempt; both were drifting toward no goal. Andersen found a meaning for life in Anna; O'Neill was to find one in 1913 in writing.

. . .

According to Agnes Boulton, his second wife, O'Neill had gotten the idea for *Chris* in late April 1918 while in New York. After his return to Provincetown, Massachusetts, and his writing of *The Dreamy Kid*, O'Neill outlined *Chris* in the summer of 1918 on five pages of his 1918–20 notebook. A comparison of the finished text with the scene and character descriptions in the notebook outline reveals that O'Neill made only minute changes, with one exception.[4]

Because O'Neill encountered difficulties with *Chris*, he turned to the writing of *Where the Cross Is Made*, the first version of *The Straw*, finishing it in January 1919, and *Honor Among the Bradleys*, a one-act play, now lost. Only after moving to West Point Pleasant, New Jersey, did he complete *Chris*, which he dated "winter/spring, 1919." As an addition,[5] he wrote the lines at the end of Act Three where Captain Jessup offers Chris his old job as bo'sun, and Chris accepts; that acceptance supports the play's comic resolution.

The text published here, including the addition, is from the typescript sent by O'Neill to the Copyright Office and registered on June 5, 1919.[6] After Tyler had received a copy of this text, O'Neill began to change it; the revision occupied him on and off until the opening. One section of *Chris* that he revised extensively was the last scene. Tyler had requested the revision, and O'Neill sent to Tyler a revised last scene in which Chris, rather than listen passively to Paul's proposal to Anna, becomes heat-

[4] The only significant change between the outline and this text is in the character of the second mate, who, instead of being Irish, grammar school–educated and insouciant, became Swedish, college-educated and reflective.
[5] It is dated in the manuscript: "April 11, 1919."
[6] It is not, however, the script used for the stage version, which does not survive.

edly involved in their discussion, and having failed to change their minds, attempts suicide. Tyler found it too melodramatic. O'Neill revised it again, but he was never satisfied with any ending to *Chris* or to *Anna Christie.*

After cutting and revising *Beyond the Horizon* in late 1919 and early 1920, O'Neill realized that *Chris*, too, still needed further revision. Although he worked with the director Frederick Stanhope and the cast in early rehearsals, family illnesses prevented his attending the final rehearsals and the Atlantic City opening. Because Tyler's request for doctoring after the opening went unheeded, Tyler himself drastically reduced the play to a running time of approximately two hours. The text used for the final Philadelphia performances probably bore only a disfigured resemblance to the original *Chris* text printed here.

This text makes available to the reading public the only surviving produced O'Neill play never to have been printed.

As O'Neill's *Chris* was dying in Atlantic City and Philadelphia, Tyler asked the playwright for help. O'Neill refused. The reasons he gave Tyler were the following: 1) the play was faulty in its subplot, the characters of Anna and Paul needing to be changed; 2) the ending was wrong and had to be radically rewritten (he had thought of rewriting the love scene to show that Paul would not reform and thus Anna would share her mother's lonely fate); and 3) his experiment (later successful in his longest plays) "to compress the theme for a novel into play form without losing the flavor of the novel" was a failure. He advised Tyler: "Throw the present play in the ash barrel. Candidly, that is what strikes me as promising the most chance of future success, both artistic and financial." That was what he wrote Tyler, but he felt Tyler was to blame for the play's failure for casting it poorly, for cutting it drastically and for trying to make it a crass popular success. It was O'Neill's belief that had *Chris* been treated sympathetically, the play would have found its public. But the damage was already done. His only recourse was to rewrite it and prove the public and critics wrong.

By April 20, 1920, he was at work on the recension; he revised *Chris* completely during that summer and sent it to Tyler in November. Tyler found *The Ole Davil,* as it was now called, overwritten. Eventually, however, he optioned it, but let his option expire. O'Neill then had the play given to Arthur Hopkins, who believed in it and agreed to produce it. Further minor revision followed, and the play became *Anna Christie.* It opened on November 2, 1921, at the Vanderbilt Theatre, with Pauline Lord as Anna, George Marion as Chris, and scenery by Robert Edmond Jones, to much public and critical acclaim, and won O'Neill his second Pulitzer Prize (*Beyond the Horizon* had gained him his first).

The acclaim, however, was dimmed by a critical cavil which held that O'Neill had written a happy ending in order to achieve a popular success. The attack on his artistic integrity so incensed O'Neill that he wrote an explanatory defense in the *New York Times,* pointing out that the characters' problems were solved only for the moment and that they would be deluding themselves if they thought otherwise; so, too, would the audience. To his friend the critic George Jean Nathan, he wrote: "The happy ending is merely the comma at the end of a gaudy introductory clause, with the body of the sentence still unwritten." The controversy, however, so soured him as to the play that in later years he did not want *Anna Christie* anthologized and regretted that he had ever written it.

. . .

In rewriting *Chris*, O'Neill decided to shorten the play, to shift the emphasis, and to darken the mood, but not to alter the character of Chris.

O'Neill shortened the play by one-third, or approximately 10,000 words, reduced the number of scenes from six to four, and the characters from nineteen to thirteen. He shifted the emphasis from Chris to Anna, who became not only the title character but the center of the action. He darkened the mood by making Anna a prostitute, who had been raped in Minnesota, instead of a well-bred stenographer, who had been brought up in England, and by making her love interest a stoker instead of a second mate: i.e., by making the play more "naturalistic" than "realistic."

In *Chris*, there is a dramatic irony in that the audience knows about Chris but Anna has yet to find out about his past and present; when she does, it will be a comic confrontation. In *Anna Christie*, there is heavier dramatic irony in that the audience learns about Anna's past in her scene with Marthy (not needed in *Chris*), but Chris has yet to find out about her past and present; when he does, it will be a melodramatic confrontation. In *Chris*, Chris's superstitious nature is exposed when he is confronted by Anna's forthcoming marriage; in *Anna Christie*, his innocence and childlike nature are tested when he is confronted by Anna's former life as a prostitute.

Because O'Neill came to believe—at least in the early 1920s—that life copied melodrama, he transformed the play from a comedy into a melodrama. The fascination for the reader is to see that transformation.

Leslie Eric Comens

Chris
Christophersen

Characters

JOHNNY "THE PRIEST"
JACK BURNS
ADAMS
TWO LONGSHOREMEN
LARRY, *bartender*
A POSTMAN
CHRIS CHRISTOPHERSEN
MICKEY
DEVLIN
MARTHY OWEN
ANNA CHRISTOPHERSEN, *Chris' daughter*
CAPTAIN JESSUP, *of the British tramp*
steamer Londonderry
MR. HALL, *First Mate*
THE STEWARD
PAUL ANDERSEN, *Second Mate*
EDWARDS, *seaman*
JONESY, *seaman*
GLASS, *messroom steward*

(Note—The characters are named in the order in which
they appear.)

The action of the play takes place in the year 1910.

Scene—Johnny "the Priest's" bar near South Street, New York City. On the left, forward, a large window looking out on the street. Beyond it, the main entrance, a double swinging door. Farther back, another window. The bar runs from left to right nearly the whole length of the rear wall. In back of the bar, a small show case displaying a few bottles of case goods, for which there is evidently little call. The remainder of the rear space in front of the large mirrors is occupied by half-barrels of cheap whiskey of the nickel-a-shot variety, from which the liquor is drawn by means of brass spigots. On the right is an open doorway leading to the back room. Down front, at center and right of center, are two round, wooden tables with five chairs grouped about each.

It is late afternoon of a day in the fall of the year 1910.

As the curtain rises, Johnny, Adams, and Jack Burns are discovered. Johnny "the Priest" deserves his nickname. With his pale, thin, clean-shaven face, his mild blue eyes, white hair, and decorous mouth set in a fixed smile of kindly tolerance, a cassock would seem more suited to him than the white apron he wears. Neither his voice nor his general manner dispel this illusion which has made him a personage of the waterfront. They are soft and bland. But beneath all this mildness one senses the man behind the mask—cynical, callous, hard as nails. He is lounging at ease behind the bar, a pair of spectacles on his nose, reading an evening newspaper.

Adams and Jack Burns are seated at the table, right front. The former is a man of fifty or so with grizzled hair, his face bloated and unshaven, his eyes puffed and bleary. His grey suit is baggy and wrinkled as if he had slept in it for nights;

his stiff collar, the tie of which is awry, and the cuffs of his shirt are crumpled and grimy; his mouth hangs open; his eyes are half shut; his head, resting on one hand, bobs up and down in a drunken half-slumber. Jack Burns, bull-necked and squat, with a battered, pushed-in countenance, sits smoking a cigarette, looking at his companion with an amused leer of contempt. Burns is middle-aged, dressed in a patched working suit.

BURNS *(Catching Johnny's eye over the newspaper, nodding toward Adams)* Dead to the world! *(He takes hold of Adams by the shoulder and shakes him)* Hey, you! Wake up! Wha's matter with yuh?

JOHNNY *(Frowning)* Leave him alone, Jack. He's been talking me deaf, dumb and blind all day. I'm sick o' listening to him. Let him sleep it off.

BURNS You? Huh! How about me? I'm goin' to make him buy 'nother drink, that's what—to pay me for listenin' to his bull, see? *(He pushes Adams' elbow off the table. The latter jerks forward in his chair, his eyes blinking open in a sodden surprise)* Say you, Adams! Rise 'n' shine! Where's that ball you was goin' to blow me to, huh? Yuh was beefin' about bein' a gentleman a second ago. Well, if y'are one, buy a drink.

ADAMS *(In a whine)* No—not another—not for you, Jack Burns. I've got the money too, but you needn't think I'm a sucker.

BURNS *(Disgustedly)* Aw, yuh're full of prunes!

ADAMS *(Maudlinly)* I'm a sport, Jack Burns, and a gentleman—and that's more than you can say—or anyone

who hangs out in this low, waterfront, barrel-house—
where I only come when I'm on a drunk—and then
only to see my old friend Johnny there—for old friendship's sake, understan'—

JOHNNY (*Irritably*) I told you you'd get him started
again, Jack.

BURNS (*With a wink at Tommy*) I'll stop him. I'll trow
a scare into him, huh? (*He turns on Adams with a
threatening fist*) Close your trap, Old Prunejuice, or
I'll hand yuh a punch in the puss that'll knock you
dead, get me? I ain't kiddin', neither. (*Adams shrinks
back on his chair in frightened silence. Burns continues
grumblingly*) Beefin' about losin' your job! Huh!
Yuh're lucky not to have one. How'd yuh like to have
mine? I gotter go down the bay on the mail boats
tonight and work mail. That's a job for yuh—break
yuh in half in a minit. You and your job! Go ter hell!
I ain't had no sleep, see? I gotter git some sleep. So
keep your mouth shut. Yuh're full of prunes, anyway.
(*He leans his head on outstretched arms*) Don't fergit
now if yuh don't wanta git lammed for a goal. (*He
closes his eyes. Adams sits staring at him with sodden stu-
pidity. Two longshoremen enter from the street, wearing
their working aprons, the button of the union pinned
conspicuously on their caps pulled sideways on their heads
at an aggressive angle*)

FIRST LONGSHOREMAN (*As they range themselves at the bar*)
Gimme a shock—Number Two (*He tosses a coin on the
bar*)

SECOND LONGSHOREMAN Same here. (*Johnny sets two
glasses of barrel whiskey before them*)

FIRST LONGSHOREMAN Here's luck! *(The other nods. They gulp down their whiskey)*

SECOND LONGSHOREMAN *(Putting money on the bar)* Give us another.

FIRST LONGSHOREMAN Gimme a scoop this time—lager and porter. I'm dry.

SECOND LONGSHOREMAN Same here. *(Johnny draws the lager and porter and sets the big, foaming schooners before them. They drink down half the contents of their glasses and start to talk together hurriedly in low tones. The door on the left is swung open and Larry enters. He is a boyish, red-cheeked, rather good-looking young fellow of twenty or so)*

LARRY *(Nodding to Johnny—cheerily)* Hello, boss.

JOHNNY Hello, Larry. *(With a glance at his watch)* Just on time. *(Larry goes to the right behind the bar, takes off his coat, and puts on an apron)*

FIRST LONGSHOREMAN *(Abruptly)* Let's drink up and get back to it. *(They finish their drinks and go out left. The postman enters as they leave. He exchanges nods with Johnny and throws a letter on the bar.)*

THE POSTMAN Addressed care of you, Johnny. Know him?

JOHNNY *(Picks up the letter, adjusting his spectacles. Larry comes over and peers over his shoulders. Johnny reads slowly)* Christopher Christophersen.

THE POSTMAN *(Helpfully)* Squarehead name.

6

LARRY   Old Chris—that's who.

JOHNNY   Oh sure. That's who. I was forgetting Chris carried a hell of a name like that. Letters come here for him sometimes before. I remember now. Long time ago, though.

THE POSTMAN   It'll get him all right then?

JOHNNY   Sure thing. He comes here whenever he's in port.

THE POSTMAN *(Turning to go)*   Sailor, eh?

JOHNNY *(With a grin)*   Captain of a coal barge. *(As if he were reciting a piece)* Captain, mate, cook and crew!

THE POSTMAN *(Laughing)*   Some job! Well, s'long.

JOHNNY   S'long. I'll see he gets it. *(The postman goes out. Johnny scrutinizes the letter)* Furrin' stamp, it looks like. You got good eyes, Larry. Where's it from?

LARRY *(After a glance)*   British—same's them I get from the old country. It's marked Leeds. That'll be in England, I'm thinkin'. Who the divil'd be writing to the Swede from England? Looks like a woman's writing, too, the old divil!

JOHNNY   He's got a daughter somewhere the other side, I think he told me once. *(He puts the letter on the cash register)* Come to think of it, I ain't seen old Chris in a dog's age. Where was he bound last trip, d'you know, Larry?

7

LARRY   Boston, he said. Up the Sound. He'd ought to be back by this. *(After a pause—thoughtfully)* That's a hell of a job now, when you come to think of it—getting towed on a rope from place to place on a rotten, dirty old tub.

JOHNNY   Captain, mate, cook and crew! Seems to suit Chris all right. He's been at it a long time. Used to be a regular, deep-sea sailor years ago when he first got to comin' here—bo'sun on sailing ships. A good one on a windjammer, too, I guess. All them squareheads is good sailors. He cut it out all of a sudden when he got back here after some long voyage or other. Never said why. Got sick of it, I guess—work too hard. He ain't so young no more. He had a tough time gettin' this job. Bummed around here broke for months before he landed it. He was stubborn. Them Swedes are when they git a notion. He wouldn't hear of going back to sailing—not if he starved to death. Funny! I used to stake him when he was broke. He always paid me back. Good old boy, Chris! Good spender, too—when he's got it. Just like all sailors, though. Throws it away on a drunk.

LARRY   Aye. He's been drunk every time I've seen him. A divil to sing that song of his, too!

JOHNNY *(Laughing)*   Oh—my Yosephine?

LARRY   He'd drive you mad with that silly tune.

JOHNNY *(Good-naturedly)*   Oh well—that's Chris. He means well.

ADAMS *(Suddenly coming to life—with loud assertiveness)* Chris is a gentleman same's you and me, Johnny.

That's all that counts. I don't care what a man is or does as long as he's a gentleman. I don't care if old Chris is only a poor devil working on a stinking old coal barge, he's a gentleman just the same. And I know it. He and I have had many a drink in your place, Johnny the Priest, sitting right here at this very table treating each other as man to man. Chris is a gentleman and a sport, and anyone that says different is a liar! Where's Chris, Johnny? I want to buy him a drink right this minute.

LARRY *(With amused exasperation)* Cuckoo! He's at it again, divil take him! Let you keep your loud mouth shut, I'm tellin' you, or the toe of my boot'll be boosting you out to get the air.

JOHNNY No more drinks for him, Larry, till he's slept this one off.

ADAMS That isn't fair, Johnny. I need a drink—

JOHNNY *(Decisively)* I said no. That goes. You've got a skin full now. And you've talked too much, too. *(He comes from behind the bar and takes Adams by the shoulder)* Come on. Go upstairs and do a flop. Take the end room. Come on. You'll feel better after.

ADAMS *(Resisting)* No. I don't want to go to bed.

JOHNNY *(Losing patience, jerks him to his feet)* Get in the back room then and sleep at a table. Or do you want me to give you the bounce outside?

ADAMS *(Whining)* No. Leggo, Johnny. I'll go—back room. *(He staggers to the door on right and goes out)*

9

LARRY *(As Johnny comes behind the bar to get his overcoat)* He's a pest, that one, with his loud gab.

JOHNNY Smart fellow, too—when he's sober. I've known him for twenty or thirty years. Used to be clerk at a ship chandlers. Left that and became a travelling salesman. Good one, too, they say. Never stays long on one job, though. Booze got a strangle hold on him. He's been fired again now. Good schoolin'—every chance, too. He's one of the kind ought to leave red eye alone. Always ends up his drunk here. Knows no one'll know him here 'cept me and he ain't shamed to go the limit. *(Philosophically)* Well, he's a good spender as long as he's got it. Don't be too rough with him. *(His overcoat on, he comes around the end of the bar)* Guess I'll be gettin' home. See you tomorrow.

LARRY Good-night to ye, boss. *(As Johnny goes toward the street door, it is pushed open and Christopher Christophersen enters. He is a short, squat, broad-shouldered man of about fifty with a round, weather-beaten red face from which his light blue eyes peer short-sightedly, twinkling with a simple good humor. His large mouth, overhung by a thick, drooping yellow mustache, is childishly self-willed and weak, and of an obstinate kindliness. His heavy jaw is set at an angle denoting an invincible stubbornness. A thick neck is jammed like a post into the heavy trunk of his body. His arms with their big, hairy freckled hands, and his stumpy legs terminating in large flat feet, are awkwardly short and muscular. He walks with a clumsy, rolling gait. His voice, when not raised in a hollow boom, is toned down to a sly, confidential half-whisper with something vaguely plaintive in its quality. He is dressed in a wrinkled, ill-fitting dark suit of shore clothes, and wears a faded cap of grey cloth over his mop of grizzled blond hair. Just now his face beams with a too-blissful happiness, and he has evidently been drinking. He reaches his hand out to Johnny)*

CHRIS Hello, Yohnny! Have a drink on me. Come on, Larry. Give us drink. Have one yourself. *(Putting his hand in his pocket)* Ay gat money—plenty money.

JOHNNY *(Shakes Chris by the hand)* Speak of the divil! We was just talkin' about you.

LARRY *(Coming to the end of the bar)* Hello, Chris. Put it there. *(They shake hands)*

CHRIS *(Beaming)* Give us a drink.

JOHNNY *(With a grin)* You got a half snoot-full now. Where'd you get it?

CHRIS *(Grinning)* Oder fallar on oder barge—Irish fallar —he gat bottle vhiskey and ve drank it, yust us two. Dot vhiskey gat kick, py yingo! Ay just come ashore. Don't gat drink no oder place. Come straight here. Give us drink, Larry. Ay vas little drunk, no much. Yust feel good. *(He laughs and commences to sing in a nasal, high-pitched quaver:)* "My Yosephine, come board de ship. Long time Ay vait for you. De moon, she shi-i-i-ine. She looka yust like you. Tchee-tchee. Tchee-tchee. Tchee-tchee. Tchee-tchee." *(To the accompaniment of this last he waves his hand as if he were conducting an orchestra)*

JOHNNY *(With a laugh)* Same old Yosie, eh, Chris?

LARRY *(With a grin)* I'll be hearin' that all night now, I s'pose.

CHRIS You don't know good song when you hear him. Give us drink. *(He throws change on the bar)*

LARRY *(With a professional air)* What's your pleasure, gentleman?

JOHNNY Small beer, Larry.

CHRIS Vhiskey—Number two.

LARRY *(As he gets their drinks)* I'll take a cigar on you.

CHRIS *(Lifting his glass)* Skoal! *(He drinks)*

JOHNNY Drink hearty.

CHRIS *(Immediately)* Have oder drink.

JOHNNY No. Some other time. Got to go home now. So you just landed? Where are you in from this time?

CHRIS Boston. Ve make slow voyage—anchor all time—dirty vedder—yust fog, fog, fog all bloody time!

JOHNNY Oh, I was forgettin'. Letter just come for you here a minute ago—from the other side. Give him that letter, Larry. *(Larry hands it to Chris who peers at it blinkingly)*

LARRY It's from Leeds, England—and a lady's writin'.

CHRIS *(Quickly)*   Oh, dan it come from my daughter, Anna. She live in Leeds. *(He turns the letter over in his hands uncertainly)* Ay don't gat letter from Anna—must be year. Ay forgat answer her last letter and she gat mad, Ay tank.

JOHNNY *(Turning away)*   Well, s'long, Chris. See you later.

CHRIS   Good'bye, Yohnny. *(Johnny goes out)*

LARRY *(Jokingly)*   That's a fine fairy tale to be tellin'—your daughter! Sure I'll bet it's some English bum ye've left back there on the street with a child on her lap!

CHRIS *(Soberly)*   No. Dis come from Anna. *(Then with a grin)* Oh, Ay gat nice gel too—kind of gel you mean, Larry. She live with me on barge. Make all voyage—everytang. Nice, fat gel. You come on board barge sometime, Larry. Ay introduce you. Ay bet you tank she's svell gel for ole fallar like me.

LARRY *(Sardonically)*   Aye. I got a picture of her. Thim kind that lives with the men on coal barges must be beauts.

CHRIS *(As if he hadn't heard this last—engrossed by the letter in his hand—uncertainly)*   Py golly, Ay tank Ay'm too drunk for read dis letter from Anna. She give me hell, Ay bet.

LARRY   A good strong lemon and seltzer'll fix you up. *(He makes it and hands it to Chris)* Drink up, now—all of it.

CHRIS *(After he has done so)* Ay tank Ay sat down for a minute. *(He goes to a table, front center, and sits down. After staring at the letter for a moment, he slowly opens it and, squinting his eyes, commences to read laboriously, his lips moving as he spells out the words. As he reads his face lights up with an expression of mingled joy and bewilderment)*

LARRY *(Who has been watching him curiously)* Good news?

CHRIS *(Pauses for a moment after finishing the letter as if to let the news sink in—then suddenly pounds his fist on the table with happy excitement)* Py yimminy, Ay tank so! Yust tank, Anna say she's comin' here—to dis country —comin' here to gat yob and live with me! She gat sick of living with dem cousins and vorking in England, she say. It's short letter don't tal me much more'n dat. *(Beaming)* Py golly, dat's good news all at one time for ole fallar! *(Then rather shame-facedly)* You know, Larry, Ay don't see my Anna since she vas little girl five year ole.

LARRY How old'll she be now?

CHRIS She must be—lat me see—fifteen year ago Ay vent home Sweden for last time—she must be twenty year ole, py Yo!

LARRY *(Surprised)* You've not seen her in fifteen years?

CHRIS *(Suddenly growing somber—in a low voice)* No. Ven she vas little girl Ay vas bo'sun on windjammer. Ay never gat home only few time dem year. Ay'm fool sailor fallar. Ven mo'der die, Ay tank it's better dem cousins in England—her mo'der's people—take Anna. And Ay stay in dis country—get yob on barge. Ay tank it's better Anna never know she gat fa'der like me. Ay vas no good for her mo'der—damn fool drunk sailor fallar—and Ay tank Ay vas no good for have little gel grow up with. So Ay stay here on barge. Ay write her letter once in vhile, dat's all. *(With a sigh of relief)* But she's grown voman now. Ay can't do her harm no more, py golly.

LARRY It's too bad her mother's dead, now.

CHRIS *(In melancholy tones)* She die ven Ay vas on voyage—twelve year ago.

LARRY And has your daughter no brothers at all?

CHRIS Ay once gat two sons—dey was eighteen and sixteen—good, big boys—sailing on fishing boat. Dey get drowned in storm year before deir mo'der die. Ay vas avay on voyage dat time, too.

LARRY *(Wiping off the bar to hide his embarrassment at Chris' sorrow—after a pause)* You're a family of sailors, God help you, like some in Ireland. This girl, now, 'll be marryin' a sailor herself, likely. It's in the blood.

CHRIS *(Suddenly springing to his feet and smashing his fist on the table in a rage)* No, py God! She don't do dat! Not if Ay gat kill her first!

LARRY *(Amazed)* Oho, what's up with you? Ain't you a sailor yourself, now and always been?

CHRIS *(Slowly)* Dat's yust why Ay say it. *(Forcing a smile)* Sailor vas all right fallar, but not for marry gel. No. Ay know dat. Anna's mo'der, she know it, too. *(With an expression of intense hatred)* Dat damn, dirty sea, she spoil all tangs. She's dirty ole davil, Ay tal you! Ay know her many year. *(Spitting with disgust)* Yes. Ay know all her dirty tricks.

LARRY *(As Chris remains sunk in gloomy reflection)* When is your daughter comin'? Soon?

CHRIS *(Roused)* Py yimminy, Ay forgot. *(Reads through the letter hurriedly)* She say she come on *Caronia*—dat's Cunard Line—leave Liverpool on fourteenth. *(Anxiously)* Vat day vas today, Larry?

LARRY Eighteenth. That's a six-day boat, likely. She'll be gettin' in day after tomorrow, then.

CHRIS *(Astounded)* So quick! *(He gets to his feet excitedly)* Py golly, dat ain't long for vait. *(Alarmed by a sudden thought)* Py yingo, Ay gat get my voman, Marthy, ashore off barge b'fore Anna come! Anna raise hell if she find dat out. Marthy raise hell, too, for go, py golly!

LARRY *(With a chuckle)* Serve ye right, ye old divil— havin' a woman at your age!

CHRIS *(Scratching his head in a quandary)* You tal me lie for tal Marthy, Larry, so's she gat off barge quick.

LARRY Tell her the truth, man—that your daughter's comin', and to get the hell out of it.

CHRIS No. She's good voman. Ay don't like make her feel bad.

LARRY You're an old mush! Keep your girl away from the barge, then. She'll likely want to stop ashore anyway, and her lookin' for a job. *(Curiously)* What does she work at, your Anna?

CHRIS She vas nurse gel, but she say in letter she learn new business. Typewriter. *(Proudly)* She's smart gel— go to school all time till tree year ago. Yust like her mo'der, she know everytang. Look at fine writing she make! *(He holds up the letter—then shakes his head resolutely)* But Ay don't vant for her gat yob. Ay don't see her since she's little gel. Ay vant for her stay with me for vhile.

LARRY *(Scornfully)* On a dirty coal barge! She'll not like that, I'm thinkin'.

CHRIS Ay never write in letter Ay vork on barge. Ay'm goin' tal her it's new yob Ay gat 'cause Ay'm sick on land. *(He chuckles at his cunning)* Dat'a good lie, Larry. Dan she stay with me sure. *(Seriously)* It's nice on barge—everytang nice and clean—nice stove and bed. Anna like it ven she see. And voyage ve make—yust nice and quiet—no rough vedder— plenty fresh air, good grub, make her strong and healthy. Ay gat 'nuff money on pay day so Anna don't have gat yob. *(Having convinced himself—confidently)* Anna like it pooty good, Ay bet.

LARRY I'd not bet on it. She'll be wantin' to work for herself and go about and see things, you'll find out.

CHRIS *(A shadow coming over his face)* Ay don't tank— *(With a sigh)* Vell, anyhow, so long's dat ole davil, sea, don't gat her, make her life sorry, like her mo'der, Ay don't vorry. And Anna don't know sea, don't know ships or sailor fallars. She live inland in Leeds most all her life. Ay tank God for dat.

LARRY But if ye keep her on the barge, ye old fool, won't that be sea for her?

CHRIS *(Contemptuously)* No. Barge vas nutting. It ain't sea or it ain't land eider. Barge ain't ship no more dan coal vagon is ship. Dat's vhy Ay like dat yob. Ay svore ven Anna's mo'der die Ay never go to sea again. If barge is ship Ay never go on her, py golly! And Ann's with me on barge. Ay look after her. *(Vindictively)* Old davil sea don't gat her ven Ay'm looking, no!

LARRY *(Shaking his head)* You're a crazy old nut.

CHRIS *(Worriedly—after a pause)* Ay must gat dat Marthy voman off barge so Anna don't see her. *(Larry snickers. Chris grins sheepishly)* Oh vell, Ay gat plenty time for dat—two day. *(He sighs with ponderous relief)* Phooh! Ay don't tank so much in long time. Gimme whiskey, Larry. Ay bet dis is last night Ay'm able gat drunk, now Anna come.

LARRY *(Handing him the drink)* Its better off you'll be— and richer.

CHRIS Skoal! *(He drinks and tosses money on the bar)* Give me oder one. Ay'm going celabrate, py golly! *(Musingly)* Yust tank, Ay don't see Anna since she vas little gel so high. Ay vonder vat she look like now she's big gel. Py golly, Ay'm glad Ay don't turn up toes and die b'fore Ay see her again. *(Hugging himself with childish glee)* Py golly, it make me happy, dat letter. Have drink on me, Larry. You celabrate with me.

LARRY *(With virtuous severity)* I never touch it. Wake up Jack Burns there. He'll be only too glad to drink with you.

CHRIS Hey, Yack! Yack! Ahoy, Yack!

BURNS *(Raises his face off his arms, blinking sleepily)* What the—

CHRIS *(Beaming)* Have drink, Yack. Ay celabrate.

BURNS *(Shaking himself to alertness and rising to his feet)* Sure. *(Then grinning as he joins Chris)* Hello, Captain. How's things?

CHRIS *(Shaking his head)* Pooty good, Yack.

BURNS Gimme Number Two, Larry. *(Larry serves them. The door from the street is pushed open and Mickey and Devlin enter and take up a position at the end of the bar. Both show signs of having been drinking. Mickey is about forty-five, short and round-shouldered, monkey-like in the disproportionate length of arms and legs. His pock-marked face, weather-tanned, has a broken nose twisted askew which gives him a grotesque expression when he grins. His eyes are a wishy-washy blue, his hair a muddy red, his voice hoarse and raspy. He is dressed in a blue coat, flannel shirt, and dungaree pants. Devlin is a lanky, loose-jointed man of about thirty-five with a lean, boney face, a hooked nose, beady dark eyes, and a bristly, black mustache shadowing a wide, thin-lipped mouth. His speech is sharp and explosive. He is dressed much the same as his companion)*

MICKEY *(As Larry comes down to them)* Whiskey—and a scoop of ale.

DEVLIN The same. *(Larry serves them)*

CHRIS *(Picking up his drink—to Burns)* Skoal!

BURNS Good luck, Chris. *(They drink)*

CHRIS *(With a childish chuckle)* Ay celabrate, py yimminy. Dis vas last night—dan Ay go on vater vagon long time. Have oder drink, Yack.

BURNS Sure.

CHRIS *(Begins to sing:)* "My Yosephine, come board the ship. Long time Ay vait for you. De moon, she shi-i-i-ine. She looka yust like you. Tchee-tchee. Tchee-tchee. Tchee-tchee. Tchee-tchee." *(He laughs and speaks)* Good song, eh, Yack? Ay learn him from Italian fallar on oder barge one time.

BURNS *(With a grin)* Great stuff. Yuh got Caruso skinned a block. *(Calling)* Hey, Larry, give us some service.

MICKEY *(Who has listened to Chris as if the voice were familiar)* D'yo mind that singin', Dev? I'll take my oath I've heard that voice somewheres before.

DEVLIN (*Glancing down the bar to where Chris stands with back turned to them*) The old squarehead, you mean?

MICKEY Yes. I've been mates with him on some hooker long ago or I'm a liar. You'd not forget a screechin' like his, ever. (*To Larry*) What's his name—the Dutchy there?

LARRY Old Chris, you mean. That's his name. He used to be a sailor once—a bo'sun on windjammers.

MICKEY (*Slapping his thigh*) Bo'sun? Chris? Now I know him and his singin'. 'Twas on the old *Neptune*—full-rigged ship, Dev. Let me get a look at his mug to make sure. (*He goes down the bar, peers at Chris' face for a second, then slaps him heartily on the back and holds out his hand*) Put it there, matey. I knew I'd seen the cut of your jib before. (*As Chris looks at him in bewilderment*) D'ye not remember Mickey on the old *Neptune* when you was bo'sun?

CHRIS (*Suddenly beaming and pumping his hand up and down*) Py golly, yes! You vas Mickey? Ay remember your face. Old *Neptune*—dat vas long time back.

MICKEY A damn long time—but I knew your singin', Dutchy. Who'd forget it?

CHRIS Have drink, you Mickey. Bring fallar with you. Ve sit at table. Ve all have drink, py yimminy!

MICKEY That's a bloody good plan. Come on, Dev. We'll sit down a bit. (*To Larry*) Bring us all a drink—whiskey—the best. (*Then as Devlin comes up*) This is

21

ole Chris, Dev, as good a bo'sun as ever was. *(They shake hands and sit down at table, center. Burns remains standing at the bar)*

CHRIS *(His head nodding—dreamily)* Ole *Neptune.* She vas mighty smart ship, dat one. Ay vas bo'sun board of her tree year. Ain't no more fine ships like her on sea no more, py golly. *(He spits disgustedly)* All is steamers now—damn tea-kettles. Dey ain't ships. *(He pats Mickey on the back affectionately)* It's yust good for see ole shipmate once again. Ay vas celabrating tonight. *(Larry brings their drinks and Mickey pays)* Bring oder drink, Larry. Den ve don't loose time.

DEVLIN Hold up. The next is mine.

MICKEY Down with this one. Here's luck, Chris. *(They drink. Larry takes glasses to refill them)* We're on the bust ourselves after a vige down to the Plate and back. We was paid off this morning—a stinkin', starvation, lime-juice tramp!

DEVLIN *(With an emphatic grunt of assent)* Aye!

MICKEY What are you doin' now, Chris? Workin' ashore? Ye have sense, then. The sea ain't what it used to be.

DEVLIN Rotten!

CHRIS *(With a grin)* Ay don't vork ashore and Ay don't work on sea, neider. Ay'm captain on coal barge. Ha-ha.

MICKEY You're jokin'. *(Larry brings drinks again. Devlin pays)*

DEVLIN Here's a go! *(They drink)*

CHRIS Bring oder drink, Larry.

LARRY You'll be fallin' on your nose, I'm thinkin'. Well, it'll be your big head. *(He goes to get the drinks)*

MICKEY *(Who has been frowning at Chris)* You're jokin', Chris—about the coal barge. *(With drunken insistence)* Tell me it's a lie, I'm sayin'.

CHRIS No. It ain't a lie.

MICKEY Is it truth, then? *(Chris nods. Mickey spits)* Divil take you! Who'd think it—a fine, smart sailor man the like of you doin' the like of that! On a rotten coal barge! Hell's fire!

DEVLIN *(Drunkenly quarrelsome)* A damn rotten job, I say, for a sailor!

CHRIS *(Gloomily)* Ay know all dat. *(Then grinning)* You don't know dat yob, you fallars. Nice, easy yob, Ay tal you. Ay gat cabin, nice and clean, no bugs. Gat own grub for cook mysalf—good grub. No one on board ship to tal me vat Ay do. Gat nice gel, too. *(He winks at their scowling, hostile faces)* She make all voyage with me. Ay tal you Ay vas captain, mate, cook and crew on board my boat, py golly! *(He tries to force a jovial laugh)*

23

MICKEY *(Disgustedly)* An old woman's job—for a smart sailor like you—gettin' towed on a rope from one dock to another.

DEVLIN *(Smashing his fist on the table)* A stinking, coal-punchers berth!

CHRIS *(Raising his voice defiantly)* It's nice, Ay say!

MICKEY *(With drunken superiority)* For a smart bo'sun of the old *Neptune*! You'd ought to be shamed to own it!

DEVLIN *(Morosely)* He never was a bo'sun. Not him! No bo'sun'd punch stinking coal.

MICKEY *(Emphatically)* He was so! Don't I know him? As smart a bo'sun as ever signed on a windbag.

DEVLIN *(Heatedly)* Not him! You're a liar, Mickey!

MICKEY *(Belligerently—starting to get up)* What's that?

LARRY *(Interrupting)* No scrappin' now, d'ye hear? Here's your drinks. *(He brings them. Devlin subsides into sullen silence. Mickey glares at Chris rebukingly. Chris pays for the drinks, shame-faced, avoiding Mickey's eyes)*

CHRIS *(Taking up his drink—placatingly)* Skoal, you fallars.

MICKEY *(Reprovingly)* I don't know as I'd ought to drink with you—and you what you are!

DEVLIN *(Gruffly)* I won't drink with him—a coal-puncher! *(He pours his drink on the floor. Chris flushes guiltily and swallows his drink, sputtering)*

MICKEY I oughtn't but—*(He takes his glass)* it's a shame to waste it. *(He drinks and fixes Chris with a sorrowful eye)* Old Chris—as smart a bo'sun as ever—on a coal scow!

DEVLIN *(Scornfully)* Calls himself a man, too!

CHRIS *(Crushed—at the point of drunken tears)* Ay tal you, you fallars, you make big mistake. You don't know—

MICKEY Mistake, is it? God stiffen you! *(Suddenly leaning over and grasping Chris by the arm—fiercely)* Will you ship away with us, Chris, when our money's gone? Will you make a man of yourself again, or stay a rat?

DEVLIN And a barge rat at that!

CHRIS *(His eyes stare at Mickey in amazement)* Ship away —on sea? *(He seems to begin to comprehend this proposition, and, as Mickey goes on, his face grows white with rage)*

MICKEY *(Intense emotion trembling in his voice)* Will you do that, Chris, for old friendship's sake—ship away to sea again?

DEVLIN *(Maudlinly)* Ship away, old Chris, ship away!

MICKEY We'll find a clean, smart ship for the three of us —when our money's spent.

DEVLIN   When our money's spent, we'll do that!

MICKEY   No lime-juice tramp this time! I've my bellyfull of steam. To hell with it!

DEVLIN   To hell with steam!

MICKEY   *(Almost chanting the words)*   We'll find a tall, smart daisy of a full-rigged ship with skys'ls—a beautiful, swift hooker that'll take us flyin' south through the Trades.

DEVLIN *(Sings)*   Oh, away Rio!

MICKEY   A sweet, slim clipper like the old ones, Chris. If there's one left on the seas, we'll find her!

DEVLIN   Aye, we'll find her!

MICKEY *(This time imploringly)*   Will you ship with us, Chris, for the love of God? Or has this dirty scow of yours destroyed you entirely? *(Chris glares at him with hatred, his lips moving as if his seething rage were vainly seeking for words strong enough)*

DEVLIN *(With a groan)*   No use, Mickey. He's damned and done for. Hell's full of his like.

MICKEY *(Shaking Chris' arm—violently)*   Answer me, Dutchy!

CHRIS *(Shaking off his hand furiously—sputtering)*   You damn Irish fallar—you vas damn fool, you! *(He shakes his fist in Mickey's astounded face and lurches to his feet)* You shut dat big mouth, py yingo! You try for gat me back on sea ven Ay'm drunk? Dat's oder one sea's dirty tricks. She try gat me back many time, dirty ole davil! *(He shakes his fist at the door as if visualizing the sea outside)* She's try all tricks on me for gat me back but Ay tal her go to hell all time last twelve year. Ay tal her go to hell now once again. She kill my fa'der, my tree bro'der, dan my mo'der's all lone, she die too. Dan Ay gat married and Ay don't see my vife only five time in twenty year. Ven my boys vas born, Ay vas away on voyage. Ven my gel, Anna, is born, Ay vas on odder voyage, too. Dan dat first voyage on ole *Neptune,* my two boys gat drowned by home on fishing boat. Ay don't never see them again. Second voyage on ole *Neptune,* my vife die in England, and Ay don't never see her again, neider. All years Ay vas at sea Ay gat drunk on pay day, spend all money, ship avay again, never gat home. Dat's vat dirty tricks of dat ole davil, sea, do to me. Dan, ven my voman die, Ay hate dat ole davil so much Ay say: "You tank you gat me next. Ay fool you yust dis one time, py yingo." Dan Ay gat yob on barge here. Ay know Ay can't vork on land. Ay'm too ole dog for learn new tricks. But vork on barge ain't on land, ain't on sea, neider. Barge ain't sea boat, Ay tal you! It ain't nutting. Dat's only vay Ay gat for beat ole davil sea. And you vant for me ship avay on sea with you fallars— yust now ven Anna come to me? Ay tal you, dat ole davil sea don't gat me no more! *(He strikes table with his clenched fist)* No, py God! No more!

LARRY *(Irritably)*   Easy, there! Don't break the table, ye old loon!

CHRIS *(Brought up abruptly, sputters and then grins)* Poof! Ay'm ole fool for gat mad at you drunk fallars.

Ay forgat Ay celabrate. My Anna's coming home. Give us oder drink, Larry.

MICKEY *(With a characteristic drunken reversal of opinion— getting up and slapping Chris on the back)* You're right, old Chris, right as rain!

DEVLIN *(Half-asleep)* Right as rain.

MICKEY *(Feelingly—on the verge of tears)* Sure, why shouldn't an old man that the sea's taken all from be shut of it and have his peace? It's a dog's life, anyway.

DEVLIN A dog's life.

CHRIS *(Again beaming with bliss—drunkenly)* Have odder drink, you fallars. Ay sing song. *(He starts to sing his Josephine song beginning in the middle:)* "De moon, she shi-i-i-ine. She looka yust like you. Tchee-tchee. Tchee-tchee. Tchee-tchee."

as

(The Curtain Falls)

Scene—The interior of the cabin on the barge, Simeon
Winthrop *(at dock in New York harbor)—a narrow, low-
ceilinged compartment the walls of which are painted a light
brown with white trimmings. On the left, forward, a small
cooking range with wood and coal box beside it. On nails in
the wall over the stove hang a few cooking utensils, pots and
a frying pan. In the rear of stove, a door leading to Chris'
sleeping quarters. In the far left corner, a locker for dishes,
painted white, on the door of which a mirror hangs on a nail.
In the rear wall, two small, square windows and a door
opening out on the deck toward the stern. In the right wall,
two more windows looking out on the port deck. White cur-
tains, clean and stiff, are at all the windows. A table with two
cane-bottomed chairs stands in the center of the cabin. A
dilapidated wicker rocker, painted brown, is placed before the
stove.*

*It is around the noon hour of a sunny day two days later.
From the harbor and docks outside, muffled by the closed door
and windows, comes the sound of steamers' whistles and the
puffing snort of donkey engines of some ship unloading
nearby.*

*As the curtain rises, Marthy Owen and Chris are discov-
ered. Marthy is not beautiful. She might be forty or fifty.
Her jowly, mottled face with its thick red nose is streaked
with interlacing, purple veins. Her big mouth is thick-
lipped and droops laxly. Some of her teeth are missing. Her
thick grey hair is piled anyhow in a greasy mop on top of
her round head. Her figure is flabby and fat; her breath
comes in wheezy gasps; she speaks in a loud mannish voice,*

punctuated by explosions of hoarse laughter. But there still twinkles in her blood-shot blue eyes a youthful lust for life which hard usage has failed to entirely stifle, a sense of humor mocking but good tempered. She wears a man's cap, a double-breasted man's jacket, and a grimy calico skirt. Her bare feet are incased in a man's brogans several sizes too large for her, which gives her a shuffling, wobbly gait. She is relaxed comfortably in the rocker in front of the stove, her eyes drowsily following a wheezing whisp of steam ascending upwards from the spout of the kettle on the stove. Chris wanders nervously about the room, casting quick, uneasy side glances at her face. He carefully turns his back to her to take a secret peep at his dollar watch, and sighs helplessly. His attitude betrays an overwhelming anxiety which has him on tenterhooks. He pretends to be busily engaged in setting things shipshape but this occupation is confined to picking up some object, staring at it stupidly for a second, then aimlessly putting it down again. He attempts to whistle a few bars of "Josephine" with careless bravado but the whistle peeters out futilely. Then he clears his throat huskily and sings in a voice incredibly doleful: "My Yosephine, come board de ship. Long time Ay vait for you—" But this reminds him of impending disaster and he abruptly stops. He is dressed in his very best, a blue suit somewhat frayed by time, black shoes glistening with polish, and an immaculate, white cotton shirt with a soft collar and blue tie.

CHRIS *(Clearing his throat and approaching Marthy's chair with the courage of desperation—stammeringly)* Ay vas expecting company come aboard barge dis morning, Marthy, and—

MARTHY *(Startled from her doze—explosively)* Wha's that? *(Then stretching herself with a sleepy grin)* Gawd, I musta been dozin' off. What did yuh say, Dutchy?

CHRIS *(Whose courage has fled at the force of her first exclamation—feebly)* Ay vas sayin'—Don't kettle bile yet?

MARTHY It will in a secon'. Yuh want some tea, don't yuh?

CHRIS *(Peevishly)* No. No, Ay don't vant nutting.

MARTHY Why didn't yuh say so before? Here I been waitin'. *(She gets up, stretching)* I'm dopey with sleep. Guess I'll beat it ashore and git a scoop of ale to open me lamps. Come on and blow me, Chris. *(She grins at him quizzically)*

CHRIS *(With haste—uneasily)* No. Ay can't. Ay gat stay aboard.

MARTHY Wha' for? *(Making as if to sit down again—provokingly)* Then I won't go on me lonesome.

CHRIS *(Eagerly)* Yes. You go. Ay give you money for treat on me. *(He takes half a dollar from his pocket and hands it to her)*

MARTHY *(Takes it—peers at him for a moment keenly, grinning)* Wha's up, Dutchy, yuh're gittin' so gen'rous?

CHRIS *(Takes her arm persuasively—forcing a smile)* You go gat drink, Marthy, dat's good gel.

MARTHY *(Shaking his hand off)* Leggo me. Wha's the rush? *(She pretends to fly into a rage, her twinkling eyes enjoying Chris' misery)* Wha' yuh tryin' to do, huh? Git rid o' me, huh? Gimme the bum's rush ashore, huh? Lemme tell yuh somethin', Dutchy. There ain't a

31

squarehead workin' on a boat man enough to git away with that. Don't start nothin' yuh can't finish.

CHRIS *(Miserably)* Ay don't start nutting, Marthy. Ay vant treat you, dat's all.

MARTHY *(Glares at him for a second—then cannot control a burst of laughter)* Ho-ho! Yuh're a scream, Square-head—an honest-ter-Gawd knockout! Ho-ho! *(She wheezes, panting for breath)*

CHRIS *(With childish pique)* Ay don't see nutting for laugh at.

MARTHY *(Pointing to the mirror)* Take a look in that and yuh'll see. Ho-ho! *(Recovering from her mirth—chucklingly)* Think I was really sore at yuh, Dutchy? It's a shame ter kid yuh. *(She slaps him on the back)* Say, wha's been the matter with yuh since yestiday mornin'? Yuh been goin' round s'if yuh was nutty, washin' and scrubbin' this dump till yuh near had me nuts, too. Think I ain't noticed, huh? Why don't yuh speak up—git it off yer chest? *(Scornfully)* A squarehead tryin' to kid Marthy Owen at this late day! After me campin' with barge men the last twenty years! I'm wise to the game up, down and sideways. I'm hep to all the dirty tricks yuh could play on me b'fore yuh start 'em.

CHRIS Dis vasn't no dirty trick, Ay svear!

MARTHY *(Warningly)* It'd better not be. *(Then kindly)* Say, lissen: I was wise to yer game yestiday mornin' at the start. I been trou the mill b'fore, and I know the signs in a man when I see 'em. I ain't been born and dragged up on the waterfront for nothin'. *(She claps the*

bewildered Chris on the back) And I packed all me duds
noon yestiday. I'm quittin' yuh, get me? Think I'd give
yuh the satisfaction of tellin' me ter beat it? Not much.
Not this chicken! I'm tellin' yuh I'm sick o' stickin'
with yuh, and I'm leavin' yuh flat, see? There's plenty
o' guys on other barges waitin' for me. Always was, I
always found. *(She slaps Chris on the back again)* So
cheer up, Dutchy! When I go ter git this drink yuh'll
be rid o' me for good—and me o' you—good riddance
for both of us. Ho-ho.

CHRIS *(Soberly)*   Ay don't tank dat. You vas good gel,
Marthy.

MARTHY *(Grinning)*   Good girl? Aw, can the bull! Well,
yuh treated me square, yuhself. So it's fifty-fifty. Nobody's sore at nobody. We're still good frens, huh?

CHRIS *(Beaming now that he see his troubles disappearing)*
Yes, py yingo!

MARTHY   That's the talk! In all my time I tried never to
split with a guy with no hard feelin's; and that way I got
lots o' frens stead o' soreheads. But why didn't yuh tell
me straight yuh was trou. Why'd yuh try to hide it?
Scared I'd kick up a row? That ain't my way. No one
man's worth gittin' sore about. There's too many others.

CHRIS   No. Ay vasn't scared. Ay yust don't vant for hurt
you.

MARTHY *(Angrily)*   Hurt me? You? *(Then she laughs)*
Ho-ho! What a chanct! At my age! *(Then regarding him
with kindly scorn)* Say, yuh're a simple kind o' guy,
ain't yuh?

CHRIS *(Grinning)*   Ay tank, maybe.

MARTHY What I can't figger, 's this: Wha's come over yuh all of a sudden? Yuh never went cheatin' with other women like most guys. Yuh're no lady killer, Dutchy. Was it some dame yuh met ashore night b'fore last yuh liked better'n me? Or are yuh just tired o' the same old thing?

CHRIS *(Hastily)*   No, don't tank dat, py yimminy! *(Hesitatingly)* You know, Ay tal you Ay gat daughter in England? *(Marthy nods. Chris scratches his head in embarrassment)* Vell, Ay gat letter from her oder night. She's —Anna's comin' to dis country.

MARTHY *(Looks at him keenly for a moment to make out whether he's lying or not—then satisfied)*   She's comin'? When?

CHRIS   Dis morning. Steamer vas due for dock dis morning.

MARTHY   This mornin'? *(Then suspiciously)* Why ain't you down ter meet her, then?

CHRIS   Ay gat no good clothes for dat. She go from boat to Yohnny the Priest to look for me, and Ay've tole Yohnny tal her, pay for carriage bring her to dis dock. She find barge all right.

MARTHY   Thank she'd mind yer clothes? Yuh're a simple nut, Dutchy. How old's she?

CHRIS   Twenty, Ay tank.

MARTHY *(Disapprovingly)* Yuh think? *(Then laughing)* Ho-ho! Yuh're a funny stiff! Say, she's only a kid. Yuh ain't goin' to have her livin' on the barge, are yuh?

CHRIS Yes. Ay try for keep her with me.

MARTHY *(Severely)* It's no dump for a kid, lemme tell yuh.

CHRIS Ay tank—it's nice.

MARTHY Nice? Ho-ho! Fur Gawd's sake! *(She suddenly assumes a bustling air)* If the boat was docked this mornin' she'd ought to be here now—if she ain't got lost by your fool directions. I'll blow outa this quick. If she ever lamped me here yuh'd have to do some explainin', huh? *(Irritably)* Why didn't yuh tell me this b'fore, yuh thickhead? Think I'd get sore when it's your kid comin'? Not much! That ain't Marthy's way. *(Scornfully)* Think I'd break my heart to lose yuh? Commit suicide, huh? Ho-ho! Gawd! The world's full o' men, if that's all I'd worry about! *(Sharply)* Heft me bag out o' there. I got a head on me this mornin'. *(Chris goes in room on left and returns with her bag, an aged rattan suitcase bound up with rope)* Now I'll be beatin' it. I ain't lookin' for no hair-pullin' with no angry daughters when I ain't in shape. Gimme a dollar, huh? I'll drink her health for yuh. What's her name—Anna? I'll say: "Here's luck to Anna."

CHRIS *(Eagerly)* Sure tang. You have good celabrate for me. *(He takes out a bill)* Ay ain't gat one. You take dis two. *(With a grin)* Dat's better.

MARTHY *(Takes it—with a smile)* Yuh're a good guy, old Chris. I on'y hope my next's as good. *(Abruptly, taking her bag under her arm)* Well, I'll be makin' a move. So long, Chris. *(They shake hands. She goes to the door)* I'll see yuh sometime someplace if yuh're still of the boats and we'll have a drink together—to show we're frens, see?

CHRIS Yes, py golly! Ve do dat for sure.

MARTHY *(Holding the door open)* And take a fool's advice and keep your Anna offen the barge. It's a bum game. So long. *(She starts to go out)*

CHRIS Good'bye.

MARTHY *(Suddenly retreating into the cabin—in a harsh whisper)* There's some dame just comin' aboard. Must be her, huh? She's comin' astern. Don't look so scared, yuh fool! I'll fix it. Leave it ter me. *(She digs him in the ribs)* I'm tryin' ter sell yer somethin', get me? *(Chris stands waiting with a look of dazed apprehension. Anna appears on the deck before the doorway, carrying a suitcase. She can just make out Marthy's figure inside the doorway)*

ANNA *(Addressing her)* Is there a Mr. Christophersen here?

MARTHY In here, ma'am. *(Then turning to Chris—in a loud tone)* I can't sell yuh nothin' for the cabin today, huh? Well, I'll try yuh again next time yuh're in port. Good day. *(She goes out, casting a critical look at Anna as she passes her just outside the door)*

CHRIS *(Faintly—in answer to Marthy)* Good day. *(Then raising his voice)* Anna?

ANNA *(Putting her head inside the cabin—uncertainly, as if the word were a strange one to her)* Father?

CHRIS *(His eyes fixed hungrily on her face—in a whisper)* Anna! *(He is terribly nonplused at seeing her so pretty, so full grown, so well dressed, so modern, so different from what his idea of her had been. He shrinks back against the wall with an air of servile deference, murmuring)* Von't you come in cabin?

ANNA *(Her eyes still blinded by the sunshine outside)* Where are you, Father? The sun's in my eyes still. It's so dark in here at first. *(She comes into the cabin and stands before him, hesitating, confused, looking at him as at a stranger. She is a tall, blond, fully developed girl of twenty, built on a statuesque, beautifully moulded plan— a subject for a sculptor with the surprising size of her figure so merged into harmonious lines of graceful youth and strength as to pass unnoticed. There is something, too, of the statue in the perfect modelling of her face. But her expression is alert, mobile, intelligent. Only her wide blue eyes betray anything of the dreamer. They shine with an eager, wistful light. Her smile reveals her father's good nature, but in her it is more detached, induced by a feeling of confident self-sufficiency. She has her father's firm jaw also, but toned down from obstinacy to strength in repose. She speaks slowly with an English accent, her voice low but distinct and clear toned. She is dressed simply in a blue, tailormade suit)*

CHRIS *(Looking about him with pitiful nervousness as if to avoid the appraising glance with which she takes in his face, his clothes, the surrounding room—his voice seeming to plead for her forbearance)* Anna!

37

ANNA *(Reminded of her duty, comes and kisses him self-consciously—then with a trace of genuine feeling awakening in her voice)* It's so good to see you, Father—at last —after all these years.

CHRIS *(Grasps her arms and looks into her face—then, overcome by a wave of fierce tenderness)* My little Anna, my darling girl . . . *kära flicka* . . .

ANNA *(Shrinks away from him, half-frightened)* I've forgotten it, Father—the old language. I have not spoken it since Mother died.

CHRIS *(Lets go of her arms and looks away)* Don't dem cousins speak Swedish?

ANNA No. They forced me always to talk English to make me learn. I had to know it well to get on over there.

CHRIS *(With a sigh)* Yes. Ay tank it's better, too. *(Suddenly reminded of the situation—with a bustling air)* Py yimminy, Ay'm losing mind. Give me dat bag. *(He takes her bag and goes into room on the left saying as he does so:)* Sat down, Anna, in dat rocker. Dat's best chair. You gat varm near stove. Ay put your bag in here. *(Anna sits down, staring about her with amused curiousity. Chris reappears)* You like some tea? Ay make some right avay—good tea. *(He winks at her, beginning to recover his joviality now that the first strain of meeting is over)* You see! Ay'm first-rate cook for ole fallar. *(He goes to the locker to get tea)*

ANNA *(Perfunctorily)* Yes, I would like a cup of tea.

CHRIS *(Coming back to the stove and making the tea)* You gat in dis morning all right?

ANNA Yes. *(Then frowning)* Why did you allow me to go to that awful dive to look for you? *(Chris hangs his head, shame-facedly. Anna continues with a trace of irritation)* Didn't you receive my letter saying I was coming on the *Caronia*? I expected you'd be at the wharf when the ship docked. I looked all over for you for half an hour. I thought I must have missed you. I remembered we might not recognize each other.

CHRIS *(With a sudden grunt of pain)* Eeh! Dat's so. Ay forgat dat.

ANNA But why didn't you meet me? Didn't you want me to come to America? Is that why?

CHRIS *(Forcibly)* No, no, Anna! Ay vant you come. Ay vant it like hell, py golly!

ANNA *(Shocked for a second—then with an amused laugh)* Father!

CHRIS *(With an embarrassed grin)* Eeh! Ay svear too much. All ole sailor fallar like me svear all time. Don't mean nutting. *(Then seriously)* Ay ain't gat good clothes for meet you at steamer, dat's vhy Ay don't come. Only gat vork clothes. Ay never need clothes for dress up, ole fallar like me. *(He gets cups from the locker. Anna's amused eyes soften with a growing affection as she watches his clumsy bustling. He pours out the tea)* Here. You take cup of tea and gat varm inside. It's chilly out in air.

ANNA *(Looking around her with an expression of amused wonderment)* You don't live here on this boat all the time, do you?

CHRIS Yes. It's nice here.

ANNA What a funny place for anyone to live in!

CHRIS *(Anxiously)* It's nice place—nice and clean—yust like home. Don't you like it, too?

ANNA But it's so small. There's no room to turn about in.

CHRIS Oh, Ay know it ain't big like house on shore, but it's pooty good for ole fallar like me *(Persuasively)* Ay tank you like him very much, too, ven you gat used to place.

ANNA And do you do all your cooking and washing yourself—right in this same tiny little room?

CHRIS *(Uneasily)* Yes. It's more easy for me dat vay. *(He gives her hand a kindly pat. She smiles up at him)* Here. You drink tea—dan talk.

ANNA *(After a hesitating sip, makes a wry face)* Ugh! Do you call that tea, Father? *(With a smile)* I see I'll have to teach you how to make tea sometime.

CHRIS *(Beaming at once)* Yes. You yust show me. Ay like learn from you.

ANNA Sometime. *(After a pause)* You never said in your letters that you worked on a boat. I thought—

CHRIS *(Lying glibly)*   Oh, Ay vork on land long time—as yanitor in house. Yust short time ago Ay gat dis yob 'cause Ay vas sick, need open air.

ANNA *(With a laugh)*   You'd never think so. You look healthy enough now. *(Interestedly)* But what do you do on this boat? What does it do?

CHRIS   Oh, yust vork about. She's towed one port for load coal; dan towed oder port for unload. Ay yust keep watch on tow line, anchor her in harbor, sometimes raise small sail, tend to tangs on deck, steer sometime —yust easy vork for ole fallar.

ANNA *(Thoughtfully)*   I remember that you wrote once, a long time ago, that you'd never go back to sea again.

CHRIS *(His face darkening)*   Yes. Ay svear dat ven your mo'der die.

ANNA   That was long ago. *(After a pause)* I can hardly remember her any more. *(Leaning forward in her chair)* Tell me about Mother, Father. My cousins never seemed to care to speak much about her. I imagine she didn't get on well with them—that one year in Leeds before she died. But she was an educated woman—a clergyman's daughter—wasn't she?

CHRIS *(Gloomily—with evident reluctance)*   Yes. Her mo'der die ven she vas kit. Her fa'der die yust couple months before she marry me. *(Slowly)* It's better for him dat vay, so he never know she marry crazy, sailor fallar like Ay vas. He vas proud, hard man. Oh, your mo'der vas smart voman. She go to school all time till she marry me. She learn everytang. *(With a sad smile)*

Only foolish tang she ever do is marry me. Ay vas vild, young sailor fallar dem day—good sailor, too—but good sailor don't make good husband, no!

ANNA *(Looking at him curiously, not knowing what to make of this confession)* But she—loved you, didn't she?— always?

CHRIS *(Flushing guiltily and trying to force a laugh)* Yes —Ay guess, Anna—but she vas fool for do it. Ay vasn't good enough, no. *(Then with great feeling)* And Ay love her, Anna—alvays—and now, too!

ANNA *(Much moved, is silent for a while—then after a pause)* You were away at sea most of the time when I was little, weren't you? I don't remember you at all. And my cousins never mentioned you. I don't think they approve of—sailors. *(She laughs)* Why, if it hadn't been for your letters, I'd never have known I had a father.

CHRIS *(Sadly)* Yes. Ay vas on deep-sea voyage all time dem year.

ANNA And my two brothers—I don't remember them at all, either.

CHRIS Dey vas drowned ven you vas so little—fine, big boys.

ANNA *(Coming out of her reverie—with a sigh)* Well, you're back as a sailor again in spite of all your promises.

CHRIS *(Scornfully)* Dis ain't sailor yob. Any ole landlubber do dis, py golly!

ANNA But it's on the sea; and you wrote how you'd grown to hate the sea, I remember. Didn't you?

CHRIS *(Intensely)* An Ay do hate dat ole davil, py yimminy! *(Argumentatively)* Dis ain't on sea, dis barge. She don't make no voyage at sea out sight of land. She yust gat towed on harbor, on canal, on river, on Sound—no deep sea—no rough vedder. She ain't ship. She's yust ole tub—like piece of land with house on it dat float but can't go no place by itself. Yob on her ain't sea yob.

ANNA *(Perplexed by his vehemence in proving this point of distinction)* Well—it doesn't matter, does it, as long as it's good for your health?

CHRIS No, Ay don't gat yob on sea, Anna, if Ay die first! Ay svear dat once. Ay keep my vord, py yingo! *(Looking at her anxiously)* You don't like sea eider, Anna, Ay bet?

ANNA I? I didn't like it coming over. I was sick most of the trip. The steerage was so dirty, and I didn't have money enough after I'd bought clothes to come second class. *(Shaking her head)* No. I've lived inland so long. I like that best.

CHRIS *(Joyously)* Ay'm glad for hear you say dat, py golly! Dat ole davil sea, she ain't good for nobody. She kill your two bro'der, she kill your mo'der, too; she kill me too, if Ay stay on her.

ANNA *(Slowly—not understanding)* She killed Mother? But Mother died in Leeds.

CHRIS *(Shaking his head—darkly)* She kill her yust the

same—by me. Ay vas avay on voyage. Ay don't come home.

ANNA *(With a shudder)* Don't. Let's talk of something else.

CHRIS *(After a pause—inquisitively)* You like sailor fallars, Anna?

ANNA I've never known one. Why?

CHRIS Dey vas bad fallars for young gel, Ay tank. *(Anna smiles)* Never save money, gat drunk in port. Ay vas sailor myself. Ay know dat gang.

ANNA *(Laughing)* Oh, Father! And are the officers as bad as the men?

CHRIS *(Forcibly)* No good, eider. Yust slave drivers. Dey're vorser'n before the mast, py golly. *(Suspiciously)* Vhy you ask about officer? You know one, yes?

ANNA *(With a laugh)* No. Why? Does it worry you?

CHRIS *(Pleased)* Vorry? Not for you, Anna. Ay can tal you gat sense.

ANNA *(More and more amused)* Thank you, Father.

CHRIS *(Sitting down beside her)* And now you tal me about yourself. You say in letter you learn oder yob—typewriter?

ANNA Yes, indeed. I'm a full-fledged typist now, Father. *(Chris looks vague at this but nods his head)* I only took a situation as a nurse temporarily. *(With a smile)* You didn't think I'd picked that out for a life work, did you?

CHRIS You don't like take care of kits?

ANNA Oh, I liked the children well enough, and the people themselves were kind to me. I was really more of a governess than anything else—a privileged character. I was allowed the use of their library and read a lot. *(Impatiently)* Oh, it was nice and homelike—and stuffy!—and it bored me to death! I'd never have remained with them as long as I did—a year—if I hadn't an end in view. I wanted the money, I hoarded it like a miser, so that when I left them I could afford a course in stenography. That meant independence—a step along the right path. Besides, our cousins are not rich and they had made sacrifices to keep me in school until I was seventeen. I owed it to them to take myself off their hands.

CHRIS You liked dem cousins?

ANNA Indeed I did. They were always kind. I was like a daughter to them. *(With the same irrepressible impatience)* But they were so religious and strict, Father—prayers morning and evening—and so old-fashioned in their ideas—and so humble—and stuffy! I had to get out of their house finally—to breathe freely. And as a typist I made enough to live on my own and be myself.

CHRIS *(Vaguely mystified and impressed by all this)* And you vorked on dis new yob over dere?

ANNA For over a year past—in a barrister's office—a first-class position.

45

CHRIS   Den why you leave dat yob? You vant travel, eh? *(Hopefully)* You vant see your ole fa'der, maybe?

ANNA   Yes, that was part of the reason, I fancy. I was becoming fed up after the novelty wore off. But the thing which made me decide was that my employer— the barrister—a man of forty with a wife and children, fancy!—suddenly took it into his head to make love to me!

CHRIS *(Angrily)*   Dirty svine!

ANNA *(Laughing)*   Father! How funny you are! *(Then making a gesture to silence him)* At first I pretended not to notice, but he wouldn't let me alone. I asked him to stop his silliness—he *was* ugly and silly—but that only made him worse. There was only one thing to do— leave. Then it came to me that I might as well make an entire new start if I wanted to get on in the world. I dreamed of the big opportunities for a woman over here in America—and here I am.

CHRIS *(Patting her hand approvingly)*   Ay tank God for dat!

ANNA *(Her eyes sparkling)*   And I'm not going to stop as a typist, either. My big hope is to work and save until I have enough to take a course in college. *(She laughs with a trace of self-mockery)* You'd think to hear me I had some big life ambition. I haven't. I don't even know what course I want to take, or what I eventually want to become. It's all—in the air. *(Intensely)* I only know I want to get away from being just a woman, to lead a man's life; to know as much as I can, and see and live as much as I can—to always

have something new to work for. I won't grow stale
—and married. I won't!

CHRIS *(Who has been staring at her face with awed admiration as if he were becoming aware of her beauty for the first
time—enthusiastically)* You know you vas awful
pooty gel, Anna? Ay don't blame dat fallar fall in love
with you, py yimminy! Ay fall in love with you too,
Ay vas him.

ANNA *(Embarrassed for a second—then with a smile)*
That's just the way he used to talk, Father.

CHRIS *(Hurt—humbly)* Ain't no harm for your fa'der tal
you dat, Anna.

ANNA No, of course not. Only—it's so funny to see you
and not remember anything. You're like a—a stranger
at first.

CHRIS *(Sadly)* Ay s'pose. Dat's all my fault, too. Ay
never come home only five time ven you vas kit in
Sveden. You don't remember dat?

ANNA No. *(Thoughtfully)* But why did you never come
home in those days? Why have you never come to
Leeds?

CHRIS *(Slowly)* Ay tank, after your mo'der die, it's better
for you you don't ever see me. And dem cousins don't
vant it. Dey always hate me. *(He goes to a window in the
rear and stands for a moment looking out at the harbor—
then he turns to Anna—sadly)* Ay don't know, Anna,
vhy Ay never come home Sveden in ole year. Ay always
vant for come home end of every voyage. Ay vant see

47

your mo'der, your bro'der, you ven you vas born—but —Ay don't come. Ay sign on oder ships—go South America, go Australia, go China, go every port all over vorld many time—but Ay never gat board ship sail for Sveden. Ven Ay gat money for pay passage home as passenger, den— *(He bows his head guiltily)* Ay forgat and Ay spend all money. Ven Ay tank again, it's too late. *(He sighs)* Ay don't know vhy but dat's vay with most sailor fallar, Anna. Dat ole davil sea make dem crazy fools with her dirty tricks. It's so!

ANNA *(Who has watched him keenly while he has been speaking—musingly, with a trace of scorn in her voice)* Then you blame it all—on the sea. *(Then as if ashamed of her thoughts, she hastily summons a smile)* Do you know you speak frightful English, Father? It's strange you don't know it better after so many years over here.

CHRIS *(This strikes him funny and he slaps his thigh)* Ho-ho! Ay'm stupid ole fallar, Ay guess. You teach me speak good, eh?

ANNA *(Laughing)* I'll try. You need it. When I begin a lesson I'll stop you every word you speak wrongly.

CHRIS *(Delighted)* Ho-ho! You stop me every vord Ay say, Ay tank. *(He starts to his feet as if suddenly reminded of something)* Py golly, Ay forgat you ain't had nutting for eat yet. You must be hungry like shark, yes?

ANNA I am—a little.

CHRIS *(Bustling to the stove)* Ay gat nice fresh eggs, bacon, bread and butter yust for you.

ANNA *(Rising to her feet)*   I'll get an apron out of my bag, and you must let me get the lunch, Father.

CHRIS *(Shaking his head decidedly)*   No, Ay don't stand for dat. *(He takes her gently by the shoulders and forces her to sit down again)* Ay'm boss on dis boat. Ay do all vork. You sat down, Anna, dat's good gel.

ANNA *(Smilingly)*   But I refuse to let you make the tea again, Father.

CHRIS *(Chuckling)*   You vas English gel, Ay tank—so fussy with tea. Vell, you make tea. Dat's all. *(He gets down the frying pan, unconsciously singing his Josephine song. Anna listens, controlling her mirth with an effort until he comes to the "Tchee-tchee. Tchee-tchee," doing his pantomime conducting with the frying pan. Then she bursts into laughter)*

ANNA   What a silly song! Where in heaven's name did you learn it?

CHRIS *(With a grin)*   Italian fallar on oder barge, Ay learn from him. *(He opens the locker door. A loud hail is heard from the dock above: "Ahoy, on board the barge!" Chris makes a quick movement toward the door)* Ay tank dat's me dey call, Anna. Dey vant move barge fadder down dock for load, Ay guess. Ay come back in second. *(A louder hail, this time in angry impatient tones is heard. Chris opens the door and bawls out cheerfully:)* Aye-aye. Ay'm comin' *(He goes out, slamming the door, and can be heard stamping about at the stern, slacking the lines, yelling replies to the orders from the dock. Anna rises, gets an apron from her bag in the next room, and takes up the luncheon preparations where he left off. She puts bacon in the pan, sets the table, etc. She is standing at the stove with her back to the door when Chris reenters, his face red with exertion but grinning cheerfully. As he looks at Anna in her apron his face beams with a great happiness)*

CHRIS *(Pretending to feel aggrieved)* Dat ain't fair, py yingo. You sat down.

ANNA No, indeed. You sit down. You're the one who's tired now—after that work.

CHRIS Ho-ho. Dat ain't vork for tough ole bird like me.

ANNA Well, sit down. I've everything started and you're only in the way.

CHRIS *(Sits down and follows her every movement with a gloating happiness—with a great sigh)* Dis vas yust like home, see you cook in my ole cabin. Make me feel good, py golly, Anna, for see you!

ANNA You've only one frying pan. I'll have to cook the eggs and potatoes together.

CHRIS *(Grinning)* Dat's vay Ay do—mix 'em all up in hash. Dat's easiest tang.

ANNA What an uncomfortable way to live! And in there, where you sleep, there's hardly room for my bag. I don't see how you manage.

CHRIS *(Fidgeting uneasily)* Oh, Ay don't need large place. Dis is nice, Anna.

ANNA *(Authoritatively)* I don't think much of this kind

50

of life at your age, Father. It's too hard. I could hear that man cursing at you from the dock just now.

CHRIS *(With a grin)* Oh, dey all do dat.

ANNA It's a shame. He shouldn't be allowed to speak that way to an old man. *(Decidedly)* There'll be no excuse for your keeping this position, once I'm at work. I know it can't be good for you living this way at your time of life. And you hate the sea so much too. I know you'd be better off someplace where you wouldn't have the sea around you all the time to remind you of the past and make you sad. Don't you think so yourself?

CHRIS *(Vaguely alarmed)* Maybe, Anna.

ANNA You've worked hard all your life, and you've recently been sick, you say. It's time you had a good rest. Let me do the working from now on. *(With a laugh)* I'm strong, sober and industrious; and two can live as cheaply as one if they make up their minds to it. We'll rent a little house together someplace.

CHRIS *(Trying to laugh it off)* Ay gat little house right here.

ANNA *(Disdainfully)* This wretched cabin—on a sooty, old barge!

CHRIS *(Squirming—with an attempt at carelessness)* Vell, ve don't talk no more about dat now, eh? Dere's plenty of time for tank of dat.

ANNA *(Throwing him a quick glance over her shoulder as she cooks)* Time? I'm not going to waste a moment. I can't afford to. I've very little money left. I read the employment advertisements in the New York papers on the boat coming over. I'm going to the city right after lunch. I shall simply have to find work at the first possible moment, Father.

CHRIS *(Stunned)* You go ashore—right after eat?

ANNA Yes. Among other things, I've got to look for a room. Why, I've no place to sleep yet.

CHRIS *(Swallowing hard—in a choked tone)* But—you stay here, Anna.

ANNA *(Turning to him in surprise—sharply)* Stay here? On board this barge? You're joking, aren't you, Father?

CHRIS No. You stay here.

ANNA But how silly! How could I even if I cared to? Where could I sleep?

CHRIS *(Eagerly)* In oder room. Ay fix it all up for you —nice, clean blanket. Ay scrub all place yesterday for you.

ANNA But that's your room. Where would you sleep?

CHRIS Ay gat mattress, blanket for put on deck in here.

ANNA No.

CHRIS *(Excitedly)* Yust suits ole fallar like me, sleep dat vay, Ay tal you, Anna!

ANNA *(Turns to the stove again, shaking her head)* No. Even if I'd consent to putting you out, I don't want to stay. These docks must be terribly awkward to get to and get from, aren't they?

CHRIS *(Not answering—sadly)* You don't like it here with me on barge—not even little bit, Anna?

ANNA *(With a laugh)* Like it? It's funny and queer enough. I like it that way—but hardly as a place to live. Do you?

CHRIS *(Dully)* Yes, Ay do. It's nice for me. *(Anna turns and stares at him wonderingly. He hesitates—then continues more and more pleadingly)* You don't know how nice it's on barge, Anna. You vait! You see! Here in dock, it's nutting. It's dirty ven ve load coal, Ay know. But you vait! Dat ain't for long. Dan tug come and ve gat towed out on voyage. No docks, no more dirt, no noise no more. Yust vater all around, and sun, and fresh air for make you strong, healthy gel. Ve go up Sound, up to Boston, around Cape Cod, Ay tank. You see many new tangs you don't see before. You like it on barge on vater, Ay'm sure you do, Anna. You gat moonlight at night, maybe; see steamer pass; see schooner make sail; see everytang dat's pooty. You need take rest like dat. You vork too much for young gel already. You don't vant for gat yob right avay soon's you land dis country.

ANNA *(Who has listened to him with growing amazement—hastily)* But I do! That's exactly what I want to do. I want to start in earning money the first minute I can. I've got to.

CHRIS   No. Ay gat money 'nuff for us two live on here.

ANNA *(As if she still couldn't believe her ears)* Do you really mean to tell me that you expected me to live on this barge with you and go on trips with you?

CHRIS *(Earnestly)*   Yes. Ay tank dat, Anna.

ANNA *(Half-exasperated)*   But, Father, how silly! How could you ever dream—

CHRIS *(Imploringly—in excited tones)*   No, Anna! Don't make fun for it! Ay tank maybe you vant stay with me. Ay don't see you for long time, you don't forget dat. Ay vant have you with me now. *(His voice trembles)* Ay'm gatting ole. Ay gat no one in world but you, Anna; and Ay'm so happy ven Ay know you come dis country. Now Ay see you yust one second—and you say you run avay again!

ANNA *(Deeply touched)*   I *do* want to be with you, Father. That's why I'm anxious to get to work so that we can have a home together.

CHRIS *(Eagerly)*   Ve do dat sometime. But please, Anna, don't go for gat yob right avay! *(As he sees signs of relenting in her face)* You vork too much. You take vacation, yes?

ANNA *(Her excited eyes plainly showing that the strangeness of his proposal appeals to her—hesitatingly)* Don't tempt me. I can't afford a vacation, Father. The trip over was my vacation.

CHRIS *(Pushing his argument)* In steerage! Dat's hell of fun for young gel! *(Insistently)* For live on here don't cost nutting. You gat yob ashore whenever you vant— smart, pooty gel like you. It's cinch. But you vait. You take one voyage with me on barge, and you see. You like it.

ANNA *(Evidently considering it seriously—excitedly)* Fancy! It would be funny—and jolly. *(She laughs)* A trip on a coal barge—seeing America! I'd almost like to, Father. It'd be such a queer thing to do, wouldn't it? But—I oughtn't—

CHRIS *(Hastily)* You come. Dat's good gel, py golly!

ANNA Wait. How long will it take to Boston and back?

CHRIS *(Evasively)* Not very long. All depend on vedder.

ANNA But how long?

CHRIS Tree veek or so, about. Ay can't tell 'xactly. But only short time.

ANNA And we'll leave here soon?

CHRIS Yes, in couple day.

ANNA And you'll promise this one trip will be your last, and you'll start living with me on land the minute I get a position?

CHRIS At end of trip, if you still vant dat, Ay promise. Ve'll see den.

ANNA *(Bends down and kisses him—with a smile)* Then I'll go. *(With an excited laugh)* It'll be such a lark! Now, are you satisfied?

CHRIS *(Beaming)* Yes, Ay'm happy so, py golly, Anna!

ANNA *(Turning to the stove)* Then that's settled. Now we'll have lunch.

CHRIS Ay tank Ay'm hungry for eat cow, py yimminy!

ANNA *(Turning on him and shaking a fork at him admonishingly)* Good gracious! Is that English you're speaking? Repeat after me or you get no lunch. I think. Say it!

CHRIS *(Chuckles—then carefully)* I think.

ANNA *I'm* hungry enough.

CHRIS *I'm* hungry enough.

ANNA To eat a cow.

CHRIS To eat a cow.

ANNA *(Pronouncing it herself with an effort)* By jimminy.

CHRIS By yimminy.

ANNA No! By jimminy.

CHRIS By jim— No, Ay can't say dat.

ANNA Yes, you can. It's easy. Listen! By yimminy.

CHRIS *(Delighted)*   What's dat? Say it again.

ANNA   What's the matter? I said it right. By— *(She screws up her mouth)*

CHRIS *(Prompting gleefully)*   Yimminy!

ANNA   Yimminy. No. That's wrong. You're awful, Father. You've got me all mixed up.

CHRIS *(Jumping to his feet with a roar of laughter)*   Ho-ho! *(He puts an arm around her waist—teasingly)* You vas Squarehead Svede just like me, py golly! *(She laughs in confusion, putting her hands over her ears as Chris bursts into the first lines of his Josephine song:)* "My Yosephine, come board de ship. Long time Ay vait for you—"

(The Curtain Falls)

Scene—Ten days later. The stern of the deeply laden barge,
Simeon Winthrop. *It is about midnight. Dense, impenetrable fog shrouds the barge on all sides, and she floats motionless on the dead calm of a silent sea. The bow of the barge is off right, the starboard bulwark facing front. Between the stern and the extreme left of stage, a blank wall of fog. The deck is about four feet above the water (the stage). In the stern, a lantern set up on an immense coil of thick hawser sheds a dull, filtering light on objects near it—the two heavy steel bits for making fast the tow lines, the wheel, its spokes glistening with drops of moisture. In the center, slightly right, of the visible stretch of deck, is the cabin, its two misty starboard windows glowing wanly from the light of the lamp inside, like two rheumy, old eyes peering into the fog. The chimney from the cabin stove rises a few feet above the roof.*

As the curtain rises, Anna is discovered standing near the coil of rope on which the lantern is placed. She has on a black, oilskin coat, dripping with moisture, but wears no hat. No trace of fear is revealed in her expression which is rather one of awed wonder. From inside the cabin comes the muffled sound of hammering. A moment later the door is flung open and Chris appears. He carries in one hand a box foghorn, worked by a lever on the side, and in the other another lantern which he sets on the cabin roof above the doorway. He is dressed in yellow oilskins—coat, pants, and sou'wester—and wears high sea-boots.

CHRIS *(The glare from the cabin still in his eyes, peers blink-*

ingly astern) Anna! *(Receiving no reply, he calls again, this time with very apparent apprehension)* Anna!

ANNA *(With a start—making a gesture with her hand as if to impose silence—in a strange, hushed voice)* Yes, Father. I'm here.

CHRIS *(Walks over to her, carrying the horn—solicitously)* You better go in cabin vere it's light. It ain't good for you to stay out here in fog.

ANNA No. I'd rather stay on deck. I love the fog. It's so—*(She hesitates, groping for a word)* strange—and still. I feel as if I were—out of the world altogether.

CHRIS *(Spitting disgustedly)* Damn fog! *(Then he pats her on the shoulder comfortingly)* It all come out all right, don't worry. In morning fog lift, Ay tank, and ve gat picked up. Tug boat come looking for us sure. *(His tone of reassurance does not ring true. He is plainly worried, casting quick glances from side to side into the fog bank)* Dey ain't nutting you gat be scared for, Anna.

ANNA *(With a trace of scorn)* Do I seem afraid? I'm not —not the least bit.

CHRIS *(Letting it out before he thinks)* Vell, if you ain't, Ay am, py yingo!

ANNA You're afraid. Why? What of?

CHRIS *(Trying to cover up)* Oh, nutting. Ay only make yoke.

59

ANNA   No, you weren't. What is it? Tell me. *(As he hesitates)* Whatever it is, I want to know it. I won't be treated like a silly girl, Father. *(As he still hesitates)* Isn't the barge safe? Is anything wrong with it?

CHRIS *(Hastily)*   No, she's all right. It's only fog vorry me.

ANNA *(Looking around her with confidence)*   I'm sure it won't hurt us. *(In an awed tone)* It's so still—and beautiful.

CHRIS *(Moodily)*   You don't talk like that, if you know her like me. Damn fog! It's vorst one her dirty tricks, py golly!

ANNA   Her?

CHRIS   Damn ole davil, sea.

ANNA *(With a sigh of weary impatience)*   Oh.

CHRIS *(Confessing his apprehension)*   Ve must drift long vay since dat tow line bust. Tide going out, too. Ve drift right out to sea, dat's vorst; and Ay tank ve gat right in south steamer track from Boston, maybe. *(Shaking his head)* Steamer don't see us, eider, in dis fog till she's right on board. Dat's tang vorry me. Ve don't vant gat run down.

ANNA *(Slowly)*   It's strange to think of other ships being on this sea. It's so still. You wouldn't think there was another ship in the world.

CHRIS *(Displeased—staring at her for a moment—gruffly)*   It's too much still, dat's yust trouble. *(He bends down over the horn)* Maybe, Ay fixed dis horn so she vork now. Py golly, Ay hope so! *(He seizes the level and pumps it back and forth furiously. The horn gives a wheezing grunt, a last gasp, and then refuses to give forth a sound)*

ANNA *(Frowning)*   Don't.

CHRIS *(Glancing up at her)*   Don't? Vat you mean?

ANNA *(A bit confused)*   Nothing—only—it makes a horrible noise, doesn't it? And it's so peaceful all around.

CHRIS *(Giving the lever a last, desperate jerk, straightens up panting)*   Don't talk dat vay, Anna. Dat's foolish business. You don't tank or you don't say it. How's a steamer going look out for us, steer clear, if ve don't make noise? She can't see us in fog. *(Kicking the useless horn irritably)* Py damn! It's queer, Ay tal you. Ain't it yust luck dis horn gat bust yust ven ve need him most? Ay try hard for fix him, too. Ain't no use. He's alvays been good, loud horn oder time. It's funny, yes. *(Shaking his fist out at the sea—angrily)* Dat's oder one your dirty tricks, ole davil! *(Then grumblingly)* Your first voyage on barge, Anna, all dis gat happen. No, it's Yonah voyage from time ve sail.

ANNA *(With a smile at his childishness)*   And am I the Jonah? Don't be superstitious, Father. The trip has been wonderful. Everything's been so jolly—and different—since we left New York. And now—drifting all alone in the fog—I wouldn't miss it for the world. I never knew living on ships was so—different from land. And the sea—I hadn't the slightest idea of what it could mean, before. Why, I'd love to work on it, I know I would, if I were a man. I don't wonder you've always been a sailor.

CHRIS *(Vehemently)* Dat's fool talk, Anna. You only see nice part so far. Dat ain't sea, Ay tal you. *(Then returning to a grumbling tone)* But it's funny, dis voyage. Sometang wrong somevere. Vyh dey put dis barge last one on tow? Oder time she's alvays first or second one. If she's first or second dis time, nutting don't happen. Ven tow rope break dat vay, dan tug know right quick, come right back and pick us up. But she's last barge dis time, and tug don't know right avay ven she steam slow in fog. Ven she do know ve're adrift, it's too late. She can't stop, anyhow, drop oder barges in fog, look for us. She gat keep dem oder barges safe.

ANNA Where were we when the tow rope broke, do you think, Father?

CHRIS Ve vas somevere near end Cape Cod, Ay guess. Dan rope bust and ve drift out on tide—straight for deep sea, too!

ANNA *(Thrilled)* Then we're out on the deep sea now?

CHRIS Py golly, Ay'm afraid, yes.

ANNA *(Drawing a deep breath and staring into the fog)* But it's so still! There don't seem to be any waves.

CHRIS It's calm dat vay sometime in heavy fog. It's luck for us, py yingo! Dis barge is load so deep, she ship big vave, she go to bottom like stone, Ay bet.

ANNA *(Not frightened—railingly)* Then we *are* having *some* good luck, in spite of my being a Jonah.

CHRIS *(Shaking his head)* Yust look at oder tangs happen. It's funny. Yust look at dat fallar on barge tree. He's drunk ven ve sail, and he heave me rotten ole tow line ain't no good. Ay know dat tow line break, Anna, if big svell come; and it happen yust like dat. Ay tal him at time, dan he curse, call me Squarehead fool, tal me go to hell, vouldn't heave me oder rope. Dan he keep drunk all voyage on bottles, Ay bet, and dis evening he's asleep ven fog come down, and ven line snap he asleep, he's too drunk, he don't know notting happen —don't give damn, eider, dat fallar don't, ve gat drowned, gat wrecked, py yimminy! *(With a sudden burst of fury)* Py golly, Ay bet you dat fallar's sorry ven Ay next meet him ashore! Py golly, Ay bet Ay grab hold his ears, knock his head on ground till he gat sense in it. Yes, Ay svear Ay beat hell of of him, py yingo!

ANNA *(Astonished)* Father!

CHRIS Oh, Ay'm nice, quiet ole fallar till Ay gat mad. Dan Ay'm not so, no!

ANNA *(Pointedly changing the subject)* Whereabouts do you think we are now, Father—near what land, I mean?

CHRIS Ay can't tal. Maybe ve're yet near end Cape. Dere's two big lights end of Cape. Maybe ve see dem, but fog's so damn tick, Ay don't know. *(He peers about him and then shakes his head hopelessly)* Ve ought for hear fog horn anyvay, ve gat near shore. Maybe tide turn and ve drift back ashore on Cape some place. Dat's all right calm night like dis. Py golly, Ay hope so!

ANNA *(Staring seaward)*   I don't. I'd like everything to stay just as it is—just drift on and on like this.

CHRIS *(Angrily)*   Till steamer run us down and ve gat drowned, eh?

ANNA *(Recklessly)*   Oh, I don't care what happens! *(Then looking at her father with a sudden curiosity)* But you— an old sailor—why are you so—so afraid?

CHRIS *(Sullenly)*   Ay'm not scared for myself, Anna. Ay've seen many storm, many fog vorse dan dis, but Ay'm still alive. Ay'm scared for you, yes, py yimminy!

ANNA *(Easily)*   You needn't be. I'm not.

CHRIS   All ole sailor gat alvays scared of sea a little ven dey gat sense. Only young fallar dat don't know don't gat scared, and dey gat drowned very quick if dey don't learn better. Dat ole davil, she don't like for fallar gat fresh with her. She kill dem fallar.

ANNA *(With a little laugh)*   So you think I don't know enough to be afraid?

CHRIS *(Nodding his head solemnly)*   You don't know dat ole davil, Anna. *(Abruptly)* Ve keep quiet one minute, Anna. Ay vant listen. *(He stands turning his head, vainly endeavoring to catch some sound)* Ay'm going up in bow, take look, and listen for horn.

ANNA   All right. I'll stay here.

CHRIS   You better go in cabin, read book. Dan you don't tank so much.

ANNA *(Impatiently)*   Why don't you want me to think? Are you afraid I'll get frightened? I promise you—

CHRIS *(Interrupting)*   No, not dat. *(Doggedly)* Only it ain't good—tank so much out here in fog. *(She turns away without answering. He stares at her for a moment with troubled eyes)* You ain't gat no hat on head, eider. You catch cold, Anna.

ANNA   I don't want a hat. The fog makes my head feel so nice and cool. *(As he still stands staring at her—with sudden irritation)* I'm all right, Father. Attend to whatever you have to, and don't bother about me.

CHRIS *(Goes to the cabin and takes the lantern off the roof. Then he turns again to Anna—uneasily)*   You act funny tonight, Anna. You ain't sick?

ANNA *(Shortly)*   No. How silly! I'm feeling better than I ever did.

CHRIS *(Gloomily—as if struck by some change in her voice)*   You vas queer gel, Anna. Ay tank maybe Ay'm damn fool for bring you on dis voyage. *(With a sigh)* Vell, you gat yob on shore—Ay gat yob, too—yust soon ve gat back to New York. Dat's best tang for you—yob in country, py yingo!

ANNA *(With a shudder of disgust)*   Please don't talk about —that—not until we do get back, Father. All those things, all my plans seem so far away now—and dead! I don't care to think of them. They're only the outside

65

of me. They don't matter one way or the other. It's too —big—out here—to even consider them. I feel—something way down inside me—something I've never felt before—tonight. *(She laughs helplessly)* But I'm talking silly, aren't I, Father?

CHRIS *(Stares at her moodily for a moment—then sadly)* Ay'm going up bow. Ay be back in minute. *(He goes along the deck on the port side and disappears forward. Anna sighs with relief when he is gone, and sits down on the coil of rope beside the lantern, her eyes fixed with a dreamy gaze out into the fog. After a pause Chris returns carrying the lantern, dragging along the deck behind him the line of the broken hawser)*

CHRIS *(Stops and holds the lantern so the light shines full on the frayed rope—in querulous tones of vexation)* Look at dis, Anna. Yust look once! All rotten, py golly! It's ole rope must be made fast on Noah's Ark one time, Ay bet! *(Indignantly)* Dats nice trick for dat fallar heave me tow line like dis! Drunk fool! Ay beat his head for him, py yimminy!

ANNA *(Impatiently)* It's too late to get mad about it now.

CHRIS Dey ought put him in yail ten year for dis.

ANNA *(Irritably)* Oh! *(Then seeing the hurt expression on her father's face, she forces a smile)* Drop the old rope, Father. It's no use crying over spilt milk. *(Patting the coil of hawser invitingly)* Come. Sit down by me. There's nothing else you can do, is there?

CHRIS *(Dully)* No. Ain't nutting Ay can do more.

ANNA   You must be tired, too. Sit down.

CHRIS *(Sinks down beside her with a sigh. There is a pause during which he stares at the lantern despondently—worriedly)* It's gatting pooty late in night, Anna. You better turn in in cabin, get some sleep.

ANNA   Sleep? You don't think I could sleep tonight, do you?

CHRIS   Ay know you must be vorried, but ve come out all right, you see.

ANNA   Worried? It isn't that. How often must I tell you— *(She bites her lips and turns away from him)*

CHRIS *(After a pause)* You gat rest anyvay, you lay down. Must be near eight bells now, Ay guess.

ANNA *(Interestedly)* Eight bells? What time is that?

CHRIS   Twelve o'clock.

ANNA   It's queer I know so little about sea language. Coming from a family of sailors, I ought to.

CHRIS   No. It's better you don't. It don't do nobody no good, know dem tangs.

ANNA *(As if she hadn't heard)* Funny my cousins never talked about the sea. I don't think I ever heard them mention it.

CHRIS *(With a grunt of satisfaction)* Dey're farm people. Deir fa'der and mo'der lived on farm in Sveden before dey go to England.

ANNA   Yes, now I remember, they were always talking about farms. It was stupid listening to them.

CHRIS   You don't like live on farm, Anna? It must be nice, Ay tank.

ANNA   No, I would not. *(With a laugh)* And you wouldn't, either. You'd die if they put you on a farm —and you know it. You belong out here. *(She makes a sweeping gesture seaward)* It's so much finer. But not on a coal barge. You belong on a ship—a real ship—sailing on every ocean—going all over the world.

CHRIS *(Moodily)*   Ay've done dat many year, Anna, ven Ay vas damn fool. Ay gat better sense, now Ay'm ole fallar.

ANNA *(Disappointed)*   Oh. *(After a pause she speaks dreamily)* Were the men in our family always sailors—as far back as you know about?

CHRIS *(Shortly)*   Yes. Damn fools.

ANNA *(With keen interest)*   Tell me about them.

CHRIS *(Disgustedly)*   Ain't anytang for tal much. It's all same fool tang every one. All men in our village on coast, dey go to sea. Ain't nutting else for dem to do. Dat ole davil sea, she kill dem all sooner, later. My fa'der die on board ship in Indian Ocean. He's buried at sea. Ay don't never know him only little bit. He only gat home in village once in long, long time. Dan my tree bro'der, older'n me, dey go on ships, too. Dan Ay ship to sea, too. Dan my mo'der—Ay ain't gat no sister —she's left all lone. She die pooty quick after dat—all lone. Ve vas all avay on voyage ven she die. *(He pauses sadly)*

ANNA *(Absorbed)* And the others—your brothers—and my mother's people?

CHRIS Your mo'der's uncle, he's vashed overboard in Vestern Ocean. One my uncles, he die ashore in hospital, Singapore. He gat fever ven his ship's dere. Two my bro'der, dey gat lost on fishing boat same like your bro'der vas drowned. My oder bro'der, he save money, give up sea, den he die home in bed. He's only one dat ole davil don't kill. *(Defiantly)* But me, Ay bet you Ay die ashore in bed, too! Ay bet you dat, Anna! Ay'm not fool like Ay vas no more.

ANNA Were all these men just sailors?

CHRIS Able body seamen, most of dem. *(With a certain pride)* Dey vas all smart seamen, too—A one.

ANNA *(With a trace of disappointment)* None of them ever rose to be officers?

CHRIS No. Ay don't tank so. *(Then shyly)* Ay vas bo'sun.

ANNA Bo'sun?

CHRIS Dat's kind of officer. He's next to mates on ship.

ANNA *(With a glad smile)* I didn't know that. Why didn't you tell me before? Tell me about it now. What does he do?

CHRIS *(After a second's satisfaction, plunged into gloom again by his fear of her enthusiasm)* Hard vork all time. Bum grub and small pay. It's rotten, Ay tal you, for go to sea.

ANNA *(Hurt)* Oh!

CHRIS *(Determined to disgust her with sea life—volubly)* Dey're all fool fallar, dem fallar in our family. Dey all vork rotten yob on sea like dog for nutting. Ay know! Dey ain't kind fallar make officer. Dey're damn fool stupid fallar don't know nutting but yust sailor vork, don't vant for know, don't care nutting but yust gat big pay day in pocket, gat drunk, gat robbed, ship avay again on oder voyage. Dey don't come home. Dey don't do anytang like good man do. And dat ole davil, sea, sooner later, she swallow dem up!

ANNA *(After a pause—thoughtfully)* And did all the women of the family marry sailors?

CHRIS *(Eagerly, seeing a chance to drive home his point)* Yes; only your grandmo'der she's only one gat sense, she don't. And it's bad on dem vomen like hell vorst of all. Dey don't see deir men only once in long vile. Dey sit and vait all lone. Maybe, every day, deir men gat wrecked, gat sick, gat drowned—dey don't know. And ven deir boys grow up, go on sea, dey sit and vait some more. *(Vehemently)* Any gel marry sailor, she's crazy fool! Ay know it! Your mo'der, she tal you same tang if she's alive. She know it! *(With great sorrow)* Dat kill her, too. It's my fault for going on sea after Ay marry her. Ay vas stupid fallar dem day. Ay don't gat sense till too late, and Ay'm sorry all year after for dat. *(He shakes his fist seaward)* And Ay hate dat ole davil, sea, for make me crazy like dat! *(He relapses into an attitude of somber brooding—after a pause)* Ay tank dat ole davil, she hate vomen, yes? She take all men avay and kill dem so's dey never go back home to vomen.

ANNA *(Very thoughtfully—saddened by his words)* It is a strange life—people who go to sea and the ones they leave behind. But I don't feel that the sea hates me—not tonight. *(Chris grunts disapprovingly but makes no reply. After a pause Anna continues dreamily)* It's funny, Father. I do feel strange tonight. I feel—so old!

CHRIS *(Mystified)* Ole?

ANNA Yes—as if I'd lived a long, long time—out here in the fog; as if I'd come back home after a long visit away someplace. It all seems so—familiar—as if I'd been here before many times—on boats—in this same fog. And yet of course I know that's silly.

CHRIS *(Gruffly)* Anybody feel funny dat vay in fog.

ANNA *(Persistently)* But why don't I feel afraid? I ought to, oughtn't I, a girl who's always lived inland? And you've told me what danger we're in. But I don't feel afraid the least bit. I don't feel anything—but—*(She gropes helplessly for words)* restful—as if I'd found something I'd always been seeking—as if this were the place for me to be—and I feel happy! *(Exultantly)* Yes—happier than I've ever been anywhere before! *(As Chris makes no comment but a heavy sigh, she continues wonderingly)* It's queer for me to feel that way, don't you think?

CHRIS *(A grim foreboding in his voice)* Ay tank Ay'm damn fool for bring you on voyage, Anna.

ANNA   But why—if I'm happy here with you? Don't you want me to be?

CHRIS *(Gloomingly)*   It ain't right kind, dat happiness, no!

ANNA *(Impressed by his tone—in a low voice)*   How do you know? You talk—queer—tonight, yourself, Father. You act as if you thought—as if you were afraid something was going to happen to us.

CHRIS   Only God know dat, Anna.

ANNA *(Slowly)*   Then it will be God's will—what does happen.

CHRIS *(Starts to his feet—with fierce protest)*   No! Dat ole davil, sea, she ain't God! *(In the abrupt silence which follows these words a steamer's whistle sounds— faint, far-off, mournful, muffled by the fog. Anna straightens herself; a tense quiver runs over her body; a glow of excitement comes into her eyes. Chris, his hand instantly raised to his ear, strains his whole body in the direction of the sound in a desperate effort to solve its significance. As the sound flows into silence, his face lights up with tremendous relief. He stutters frantically with a joy bordering on hysteria)* Tug boat! Tug boat vistle! Ay know him, py golly! She come look for us, Anna! Pick us up! All's vell! Ve fetch Boston in morning. You take train back to New York. Gat yob. No more voyage for you, py yimminy! It ain't good for you on sea, no! *(He shuffles his feet in a kind of grotesque dance and sings with wild joy:)* "My Yosephine, come board de ship. Long time Ay vait for you. Tchee-tchee. Tchee-tchee."

ANNA *(Who, at the first mention of the tug boat, has bent forward in a dejected, listless attitude, puts her hands over her ears—in sharp annoyance)* Please stop that, Father! *(He stops, open-mouthed. She adds vehemently)* I hate that silly song! *(Then apathetically)* It is the tug boat looking for us, you think?

CHRIS Ay'm sure. Must be tug boat. She's closer dan she sound, too. Vind blow sound away from us.

ANNA *(Half to herself—bitterly)* So it's all going to end —like that!

CHRIS Ssshh! Time ve hear oder vistle. *(They listen. After a moment the same whistle is heard, perceptibly louder and clearer. As the sound dies away, Chris' expression falls into gloom again)*

ANNA *(Watching his face—eagerly)* Well? Is it—?

CHRIS *(Shaking his head)* No. Ay make mistake. Ain't tug boat. *(With terrified bewilderment)* Ay vas sure—but no—ain't tug boat—no—py damn—Ay know dat now. *(He stands as if facing this new situation had benumbed his body)*

ANNA *(Her voice thrilling once more with life and energy— springing to her feet)* Then what can it be, do you think?

CHRIS *(His voice trembling)* Steamer vistle—big steamer. *(Appalled, as if he hadn't thought of this before)* Ve're in her course! She's coming dis vay! Ve're in track! *(Overcome with terror)* She don't know ve're here. Ve gat make noise, py God! *(He pounces down on the foghorn,*

73

pumping the lever back and forth frenziedly, forgetting in his terror that this is useless)

ANNA *(In a calm tone of command)* Stop that, Father! *(He stops and stares up at her stupidly)* You know the horn is broken. Don't get so excited. *(She lays her hand on his shoulder reassuringly)*

CHRIS *(Brought back to himself, gets to his feet—dully)* Ay vas sure it's tug boat. *(Hanging his head sheepishly with a shamed side glance at his daughter)* You tank Ay'm big coward, Anna, for gat scared dat vay?

ANNA *(Quickly)* No. You were excited, that's all. *(Chris lifts his head with a relieved expression and is about to speak when Anna lifts her hand warningly)* Ssshh! *(The whistle sounds again with a loud full note)*

CHRIS *(Shocked this time into an instant, calculated activity)* She's bearing down fast, py golly! She pass close by. *(He grabs up his lantern and strides with quick heavy steps astern. He points to one of the steel bits to which a small rope is made fast)* Look, Anna! *(Commandingly, as she remains motionless, staring spellbound out into the fog)* You look here quick, Anna! Ve ain't gat time for dream now, py golly! Dat steamer run us down, maybe, py yimminy!

ANNA *(Aroused—running to his side—excitedly)* What is it, Father?

CHRIS *(Taking hold of rope)* You see dis rope?

ANNA Yes, Father.

CHRIS   It's painter—painter of small boat. Ay launch her early in night ven you vas in cabin. Ay don't tal you for fear Ay make you scared. *(Holding his lantern over the stern on the far (port) side)* See. She's all right. Ay fix her so's ve gat away if anytang happen to barge. Ay put in tinned meat, cracker, plenty vater. She's all right. *(He strides back to the bit)* Look, Anna! Ay make half turn on painter. She's easy for cast off dat vay, see? *(He illustrates)*

ANNA   Yes, Father, I see.

CHRIS   If anytang happen you cast dis off. You tumble over side ven Ay yell to you. You gat in boat damn quick, you hear? You push off, you find oars in her, you row avay like hell, you hear?

ANNA *(Protestingly—her voice frightened for the first time)* But you? I won't go till you—

CHRIS *(Fiercely)*   Don't vait for me, you hear! *(The whistle of the steamer sounds again seemingly very much nearer this time)*

ANNA *(With a startled gasp)*   Oh!

CHRIS   She's pooty close, by golly! She steam full speed ahead, Ay tank—take chance. Dey don't care for poor davil like us. *(Grasping her arm as he turns away)* You stay here, Anna. Don't move one step now! *(He strides toward the cabin)*

ANNA *(A bit hysterically)*   Where are you going?

CHRIS   In cabin. Gat life preserver. You vait. *(He disappears in the cabin but returns almost immediately with two life preservers)* Here! You gat dis on you. *(He adjusts it on her with quick, capable fingers)* Dere! You're all right. You halp me, now. *(She helps him get his on. Her hands tremble as she fumbles awkwardly with the straps. He pats her on the back reassuringly)* Don't gat scared, Anna. Keep your head now! Maybe dat steamer don't—but if she do, you yump quick, Anna, gat in boat. Ain't no time for stop, tank. *(The steamer's whistle sounds again, close on the port side)*

ANNA *(With a gasp)*   But you? I won't get in the boat without you.

CHRIS *(Roughly)*   Shut up! No time for talk more. You do vat Ay tal you, Anna. *(Then more kindly)* Ay'm all right. Ay gat stay on ship till Ay know she's lost for sure. Dan Ay yump over side. You pick me up in boat. *(He puts the end of the painter in her hand)* Remember! Ven Ay yell, you cast off and yump in boat. Ay gat go now. Ay vave light, maybe dey see it. *(He hurries to the cabin)*

ANNA *(Fearfully—in a trembling whisper)*   Father!

CHRIS *(Clambers to the roof of the cabin and peers out to port)* Ay can't see no lights. *(He swings the lantern in a circle over his head. The steamer's whistle again sounds, this time seeming to boom out of the fog right over the barge. Chris waves the lantern frenziedly and curses)* Py God! Dem damn fools! *(Then he sets the lantern down and, forming a megaphone with his two hands, shouts stridently:)* Ahoy! Ahoy dere! Ahoy on board steamer! *(As through a sudden break in the fog a loud noise of throbbing engines and swishing waves sweeps over the barge. Chris' face is turned toward the bow. He gives a loud yell of angry dismay)* Dere she come! She hit us on port bow sure! Cast off, Anna! *(Lantern in hand, he jumps to the deck and leaps madly astern to where the white-faced Anna stands with the painter she has freed from the bit in her hands. He snatches it from her)* Good gel! *(He grabs her in one arm around the waist, letting the lantern go, and slings her over the port side like a bag of meal)* Over with you! *(A thin wail sounds from the fog overhead: "Barge dead ahead!")* Chris stands with one foot on the port bulwark, ready to jump, his eyes turned toward the bow. A prolonged, ear-racking blast of the steamer's whistle seems to shatter the fog to fragments

as

(The Curtain Falls)

Scene—The main cabin on board the British tramp steamer
Londonderry—*a quadrangular room with a row of portholes on the right looking out toward the bow of the ship.
Beneath the portholes, a long bench with cushions. In front of
the bench, a large table with a lighted, green-shaded reading
lamp in the center. In the rear wall, several portholes looking
out to port. In the left wall, two doors opening on the officers'
quarters and, past them, to the bridge deck beyond. Against
the wall between the doors, a lounge. Several chairs are placed
near the table. A large, dark-colored rug covers most of the
floor.*

*The time is in the half hour immediately following the
running down of the barge by the* Londonderry.

*As the curtain rises, Captain Jessup enters from the door-
way in rear. He is a slim, well-knit man of sixty or so with
iron-grey hair, beard and mustache. His voice is high-pitched
and shrill, with a querulous, irritated quality which is belied
by his good-humored smile, and the kindly expression of his
keen blue eyes. His immaculate, well-fitting uniform gives
him the general, dapper aspect of a naval officer. He speaks
back to some one who is following him—irritably)* A loaded
barge—we were right aboard of her in the fog before you
could say Jack Robinson.

MR. HALL *(Follows his chief into the cabin, his eyes still
blinking with sleep, buttoning up his coat as if he were just
finishing dressing. He is a tall, spare man of middle age,
with a long, gaunt clean-shaven face. His thin-lipped,
wide mouth seems perpetually in a grim determination not*

to smile and to utter as few words as possible. His uniform is old and shiney. He mutters drowsily in answer to the captain) They'd just given me a call for the watch, sir. I was turning out—half-asleep—when the smash came.

CAPTAIN JESSUP   This damn fog! Bad as the Channel! No horn, no lights, no warning of any sort—and there she was dead ahead! Just time to throw the wheel hard a-port and—bang!—we were into her. We'd slowed down a minute before, though. Lucky!

HALL *(With awakening concern)*   A hard hit, sir?

CAPTAIN JESSUP   No. Not to appearances, at least. Andersen is forward having a look. Glancing blow on the starb'rd quarter. Enough to finish the scow, though. She heeled over and went down like a rock, I believe. Loaded deep. A stroke of fortune we didn't hit her full on or— *(He shrugs his shoulders)* we'd have been damned unlucky, too.

HALL   I thought I heard Andersen getting a boat lowered.

CAPTAIN JESSUP *(Disgusted)*   Yes—had to do it. One of the men reported having seen a small boat almost alongside right after we hit. Two men in it. They hailed us, too. Oh yes, plenty of hails when it was too late! Not a second before. Couldn't leave the beggars adrift, though. So—stopped.

HALL   Will we have to put back to Boston, sir?

CAPTAIN JESSUP   Dammit, no! The damage won't be serious enough to warrant that. Can't be. You'll see. Nothing so bad that we can't patch up at sea and keep our course. Temporary repairs'll do. By Jove, they'll have to! Now we're at sea, we'll keep at sea, Hall.

HALL Yes, sir.

CAPTAIN JESSUP Hmmph! You'd better get forward. Have a look at things and see what you think. And set her going on her course as soon as those beggars are aboard.

MR. HALL Yes, sir. *(He turns to go)*

CAPTAIN JESSUP Oh, and tell the steward I want him, will you?

HALL Yes, sir. *(He goes out. The captain paces back and forth nervously. A moment later the steward appears in the doorway, rear. He is a thin, undersized young fellow whose weak, characterless face wears a look of ingratiating servility. A suggestion of feeble blond mustache fringes his upper lip. He coughs respectfully to attract the captain's attention)*

CAPTAIN JESSUP Oh, Steward. Have they picked up those barge beggars yet?

THE STEWARD They're bringing them alongside now, sir, I think. I heard their voices. Sounded quite close up, sir.

CAPTAIN JESSUP *(Grimly—as if speaking aloud to himself)* Drunk, I suppose—and forgot to blow any horn. A nice go! Well, we'll make the beggars sweat for their passage down to give them a lesson.

THE STEWARD *(Concealing a smile—volunteers the informa-tion apologetically)* One of them—seems to be a woman, sir.

CAPTAIN JESSUP Eh? What's that? A woman?

THE STEWARD Yes, sir.

CAPTAIN JESSUP What would a woman be doing on that tub? You must be mistaken.

THE STEWARD *(Noncommittally—fearing he has put his foot in it)* Perhaps I'm wrong, sir.

CAPTAIN JESSUP *(Irritably)* What made you think— How do you know, eh?

THE STEWARD One of the voices sounded like a woman's, sir.

CAPTAIN JESSUP Oh, that—voices in fog—may sound like anything *(But he shakes his head, muttering with half-amused vexation)* A woman—hmmph! Some drunken slut, too, I'll wager—a barge woman! Eh, well— *(He notices the steward still waiting and is brought back to himself)* Oh yes, what I wanted you for. The beggars may have taken a wetting over board. They'll need coffee—something hot. Turn out the cook—or—see to it, eh?

THE STEWARD Yes, sir.

CAPTAIN JESSUP And tell them to bring the barge— hmmph—persons in to me here. I'll want to have a look at them at once.

THE STEWARD   Yes, sir. *(He goes out. The captain resumes his pacing. Paul Andersen appears in the doorway, left rear. He is a tall, broad-shouldered, blond young fellow of about twenty-five with a strong-featured, handsome face marred by a self-indulgent mouth continually relaxed in a smile of lazy good humor. His blue eyes, large and intelligent, have a dreamy, absent-minded expression. His low deep voice drawls a little as he speaks. He is dressed in the simple blue uniform of a second mate)*

ANDERSEN   I've had a look up for'ard, sir.

CAPTAIN JESSUP   Eh, well? How does it look?

ANDERSEN   No harm done, sir, to speak of. No leak anywhere that I could find. A few of the plates to starb'rd are bent in a bit. That seems to be all, sir.

CAPTAIN JESSUP *(Rubbing his hands together with a grunt of satisfaction)*   Hmmph! That's good, Andersen. That's excellent, eh? I was afraid we might have to put back to Boston for repairs. No end of a nasty business, that! No end of explanation to make on all sides. Not our fault, though. They couldn't say that. No horn, no lights, nothing!

ANDERSEN *(Amused at the captain's warmth—with his lazy smile)*   Yes, sir. They could hardly blame us.

CAPTAIN JESSUP *(Abruptly)*   She's on her course again. Those barge beggars must be on board, eh?

ANDERSEN   Yes, sir. The steward said you wanted to see them. They're waiting on deck.

CAPTAIN JESSUP   Tell them to come in. *(As Andersen turns to the door)* Oh—the steward was saying he thought one of them was a woman?

ANDERSEN   Yes, sir.

CAPTAIN JESSUP *(Disgustedly)*   I was hoping he was mistaken. You've seen—the lady?

ANDERSEN   Yes, sir. I talked with her for a second.

CAPTAIN JESSUP   Some drunken wench, I suppose?

ANDERSEN *(Smiling)*   No, sir—not exactly.

CAPTAIN JESSUP   Eh? A barge woman!

ANDERSEN *(With a laugh)*   Oh, I know the kind they usually are. But she isn't that. She's the daughter of the old Swede on the barge. It seems she was keeping him company on this one trip for the fun of the thing.

CAPTAIN JESSUP   Fun! A likely story! Even so—what kind of girl—daughter of a barge hand!

ANDERSEN   I don't know. I only spoke with her a second. But you'll be surprised, sir, when you see her. She seems very well educated. Spoke correct English without any accent. *(He smiles)* And as far as looks go—she's a corker.

CAPTAIN JESSUP *(With a twinkle in his eye)*   Aha! That's a reason for standing up for her, what? Well, let me have a look at beauty in distress. Tell them to come in.

ANDERSEN   Yes, sir. *(He goes out and can be heard calling:)* This way, please. *(A moment later Anna enters, followed by her father and Andersen. Once inside, after a quick glance at the captain, Anna stands hesitatingly. She does not seem embarrassed but looks about the room with eager curiosity. Chris pulls off his sou'wester as he enters, and stands awkwardly, turning it over in his hands. His eyes avoid the captain. He is full of an old sailor's uneasiness at being called before the Old Man. Andersen remains by the door, observing every move of Anna's with a greedy admiration)*

CAPTAIN JESSUP *(The stern frown he has prepared for their reception disappears as his eyes meet Anna's. He is plainly astounded by her appearance and becomes embarrassed in his turn. Finally he points to a chair by the table)* Hmmph! Won't you—er—sit down, Miss—?

ANNA *(With smiling assurance)* Thank you, Captain. *(She sits down)*

CAPTAIN JESSUP *(More than ever taken aback by the unexpected refinement of her tone)* Sorry this—unfortunate accident—couldn't be avoided, you know. Fog so cursed thick, couldn't see your hand before you. No horn, you know. *(Angry at himself for this blundering explanation, he turns furiously on Chris)* You, bargee! Why didn't you keep your horn going, eh, you idiot? Were you drunk—or asleep—or what?

CHRIS *(Humbly)* Horn vas broke, sir. Ay try for fix him but Ay can't gat him vork. He vas alvays good, loud horn before dis time.

CAPTAIN JESSUP   Bah! Excuses! Damn carelessness, that's what! Too lazy to fix it, I'll wager.

ANNA *(Indignantly)*   My father is telling the truth, Captain. He did his best to repair the horn; and he waved a lantern from the roof of the cabin and shouted to you. But you were coming so fast through the fog— *(The captain starts at this and glances uneasily at Andersen, who puts his hand to his face to hide a smile)*

CAPTAIN JESSUP *(Clearing his throat—testily)*   Not fast, young lady. Nothing of the sort. We were feeling our way carefully. Never expected— *(He turns to Chris)* How did your tub get out here, eh? Where's the rest of the tow?

CHRIS   Tow rope part and ve gat adrift in fog about four bells in evening, sir. Ve vas last barge on tow of four, so tug can't stop look for us, Ay guess. *(Eagerly explaining)* Crazy, drunk fallar on oder barge heave me rotten tow line, sir. Ay tal him it's rotten and he say—

CAPTAIN JESSUP *(Sharply)*   Never mind that. It's none of my business how you came to get adrift *(He sits down at the table and takes a notebook and pencil from his pocket)* What was the name of your tub?

CHRIS   *Simeon Winthrop*—load with coal, New York for Boston, sir.

CAPTAIN JESSUP *(Writing)*   Coal—New York for Boston. *(He makes a few other notes then replaces book and pencil in his pocket, and looks up, taking Chris' measure with a keen eye)* You're an old deep-sea sailor, aren't you?

You've not worked on barges all your life by the cut of you.

CHRIS   Ay vas sailor on deep-sea many year, sir. *(With pride)* Ay don't never vork on steam. Ay vas bo'sun on vindyammer.

CAPTAIN JESSUP *(With appreciation)*   Good. We can use you. I suppose you're willing to work your passage down, eh?

CHRIS *(Pleadingly)*   If you could put us ashore end of Cape, sir—

CAPTAIN JESSUP *(Impatiently)*   We left Cape Cod astern long ago. Do you think we'll turn back for you, eh? No, this'll teach you to be careless next time. You'll work your way down, my man, and no shirking about it either. And then we'll turn you over to your consul.

CHRIS *(Pointing to his daughter)*   Ay vasn't thinking for mysalf, sir. Ay ain't scared for vork, sir. But Anna—

CAPTAIN JESSUP *(Starts as if he had forgotten all about her—staring at her in perplexity)*   Hmmph! The devil!

ANNA *(Eagerly)*   Oh, you mustn't turn back for me, Captain. Just put me anywhere. I can sleep on deck if need be.

CHRIS *(Angrily)*   Anna!

ANNA *(Her face flushed with excitement)*   And, after all, there's nothing to keep me in America. I'd only arrived from England a short time ago—to see my father. I was taking this one trip on his barge—as a vacation—for a lark—and—

CAPTAIN JESSUP *(Surprised)*   From England?

ANNA   Yes. Although I was born in Sweden I was brought up by relatives in Leeds. Afterward, I worked as a typist there.

CAPTAIN JESSUP *(His face clearing now that he knows her exact status)*   Ah—a typist indeed. *(Then he smiles)* But, with all due respect to your calling, I don't see how we can make use of it on this ship.

ANNA   But I can work at anything. I can cook, and wash dishes, and sweep—

CAPTAIN JESSUP   I'm afraid those positions are already filled. No, Miss—er—

ANNA   Christophersen.

CAPTAIN JESSUP   Miss Christophersen. I think you'll have to be content to remain a passenger. Your father can do enough work for the two passages. As to finding fit quarters for you, I don't know how we'll manage.

ANDERSEN *(Eagerly)*   She can have my cabin, sir. I'll have the steward get my things out at once, and I'll bunk in with the Fourth. He won't mind, under the circumstances.

CAPTAIN JESSUP *(Snapping him up)*   Then that's settled.

ANNA *(Quickly)*   Oh, no. I'm very grateful but I couldn't think of putting out Mr.—

CAPTAIN JESSUP   Mr. Andersen doesn't mind, I'm sure. And you've no choice, you know.

ANDERSEN *(Smiling and looking Anna boldly in the eyes)* Not a bit of it! It's a pleasure, Miss Christophersen.

ANNA *(Flushing and dropping her eyes)* Then—thank you. You're very kind.

ANDERSEN *(A touch of triumph in his drawling tones)* Not at all. *(His glance turns to Chris, who has been watching this handsome second mate with a dislike which has turned to immediate jealous hatred as he notices the impression made upon Anna. Andersen senses this feeling on the father's part and frowns. He speaks to Chris in a tone of command)* You'll find a bunk up in the fo'c's'tle.

CHRIS *(Sullenly)* Yes, sir. *(But he stubbornly holds his ground, his eyes fixed on Anna)*

CAPTAIN JESSUP *(Carelessly)* We'll leave Mr. Hall to decide about him.

ANDERSEN *(Turning to the door)* I'd better go look up the steward and have him get my things out of that cabin. *(With a look at Anna which again causes her to drop her eyes)* Miss Christophersen must be tired.

ANNA   Oh, no. Don't trouble. I'm not tired—not a bit.

CAPTAIN JESSUP   Yes. Better see to it, Andersen.

ANDERSEN   Yes, sir. *(He goes out, smiling back at Anna over his shoulder)*

CAPTAIN JESSUP *(After a slight pause)* You're dry, eh? I mean, you didn't get a wetting over the side?

ANNA No, Captain. We were safe in the small rowboat.

CAPTAIN JESSUP *(With a grunt)* Lucky! *(Mr. Hall enters from the doorway, left rear. The captain turns to him)* Eh, Hall? Well? No damage, eh? Nothing to get excited about, what?

HALL Starb'rd plates bent in a little. That's all, sir.

CAPTAIN JESSUP *(Rubbing his hands together gleefully)* Good! We're fortunate, eh?

HALL Yes, sir. *(He turns to go out again)*

CAPTAIN JESSUP One minute, Hall. *(He waves his hand to indicate Chris)* This man—Christophersen—bo'sun on windbags for years, he says—put him to work tomorrow.

HALL *(Measuring Chris with a calculating eye)* Glad to get him, sir. I'll put him on as a day man.

CAPTAIN JESSUP Better take him up for'ard, eh? See that he gets a bunk in the fo'c's'tle.

HALL Yes, sir. *(He beckons to Chris)* Come on.

CHRIS *(Looks from him to the captain to Anna with a dazed, stupid expression on his face—stammeringly)* Ay tank— *(He mumbles in a silly bewilderment)*

HALL *(Gruffly)* Never mind what you think. Come on.

CHRIS *(Abjectly)*   Yes, sir. *(He turns to follow Hall, casting a pleading glance at Anna)*

ANNA *(Quickly)*   You'll come back to say good night after you're settled, won't you, Father? *(Chris does not answer but looks at the captain. The latter frowns impatiently. Hall's lips part in a sardonic grin)* You'll permit that, won't you, Captain?

CAPTAIN JESSUP *(Flustered)*   Yes—under the circumstances. Tonight, yes—let him come. *(Then irritably)* But kindly don't make any such requests in future. You'll see him on deck, after working hours, quite enough. *(Frowning authoritatively)* There's such a thing as discipline on a ship, young lady.

ANNA *(Smiling at him gratefully)*   Thank you so much, Captain. You're so kind. *(The captain clears his throat importantly but he feels that the wind has been taken from his sails. Anna turns to her father)* So be sure and come back, Father.

CHRIS *(Dully)*   Yes, Anna. Ay come back.

HALL *(Impatiently)*   Come along now. *(Chris slowly follows him out)*

CAPTAIN JESSUP *(Fidgeting with embarrassment now that he is alone with Anna)*   Er—you must pardon me for insisting—that matter—Miss Christophersen. Captain's cabin, you know. Members of the crew—no business here. Bad for discipline. Create ill feeling. Make it harder for him up for'ard with the others, too. They wouldn't like it. Well—you understand—they're like children. Very like.

ANNA Yes, I think I understand, Captain. I won't ask it again, now that you've told me. *(After a pause—with excited curiosity)* What is the name of your ship, Captain, and where is she going?

CAPTAIN JESSUP She's the *Londonderry*, Boston for Buenos Aires.

ANNA *(musingly)* Buenos Aires. That's a long way off, isn't it?

CAPTAIN JESSUP Six thousand miles, more or less.

ANNA *(Her eyes glowing)* Six thousand miles at sea— without a stop?

CAPTAIN JESSUP Yes. You're in for nearly a month of nothing but water.

ANNA *(With excited pleasure)* What a wonderful trip! *(Smiling at the captain)* Oh, Captain, I'm so glad— it happened! *(She laughs)* Does that sound silly of me?

CAPTAIN JESSUP *(Smiling)* Well, after a coal barge, I suppose the *Londonderry*'s not so bad. *(As he is speaking Andersen comes in, left rear. He carries a cup of steaming coffee in his hand which he brings to Anna)*

ANDERSEN Here's something to warm you up. The steward was busy changing me so I thought I might as well bring it.

ANNA *(Flushing with pleasure)* Thank you.

ANDERSEN *(Smiling down at her upturned face)* Look out. It's hot.

CAPTAIN JESSUP I'll take a turn on the bridge, I think—smoke a cigar. Don't feel sleepy. That business still has me jumpy. Narrow escape, by Gad! I'll have a look up for'ard, too, I believe—not that I doubt your word. *(He walks to the doorway, left rear, making a motion to Andersen to follow him. He speaks in a low tone)* I leave it to you, Andersen, to see the steward has her fixed up all right.

ANDERSEN *(With his lazy smile)* I'll see that she's comfortable, sir.

CAPTAIN JESSUP *(Struck by something in the other's manner)* No monkey business, now, Andersen.

ANDERSEN *(With a laugh)* Of course not, sir.

CAPTAIN JESSUP *(With half-amused severity)* Mind! *(He goes out. Andersen comes over and sits down in a chair beside Anna)*

ANDERSEN You're forgetting your coffee. Better drink it while it's hot. *(He laughs)* Pardon me, did I call it coffee? Well, anyway, it tastes good when you're cold.

ANNA *(Avoiding the direct gaze of his eyes and sipping her coffee—shyly)* It *is* good.

ANDERSEN *(Watching her with an admiring smile)* You're certainly a cool customer, for a girl, if you'll excuse my saying so. Aren't you frightened—or nervous—or disturbed the least bit?

ANNA *(Smiling at him confidently)* No. Why should I be?

ANDERSEN But weren't you scared when you heard us in the fog getting nearer and nearer—when you saw us looming up on top of you?

ANNA I did feel—queer—for a moment, but I knew it would come out all right.

ANDERSEN *(Puzzled)* You knew? How?

ANNA *(Vaguely)* I can't explain it. I simply felt sure. It didn't seem as if I'd been made to be drowned tonight, that's all.

ANDERSEN You were close to it, though. It was only the merest luck.

ANNA *(Indifferently)* Yes, I suppose we were in great danger.

ANDERSEN *(With a low chuckle)* Danger? You *suppose*?

ANNA *(Wrinkling her brows in the effort to express what she feels)* But, at the same time, I *felt* there was no danger. I knew it couldn't be the end of everything—so soon. Somehow—I can't explain what I mean—something— perhaps it was the sea—I don't know what—told me that it was a new beginning of my life, not an end.

ANDERSEN *(Curiously)* And you still think that?

ANNA *(Nodding her head emphatically)* Oh, yes. Now more than ever.

ANDERSEN *(With a laugh)* Then you must be glad you were shipwrecked?

ANNA *(Smiling)* Indeed I am. Otherwise this— *(She makes a gesture to indicate the ship)* could never have happened.

ANDERSEN And you've no regrets?

ANNA Regrets?

ANDERSEN For what you've left behind?

ANNA Oh, I've left nothing behind. I've only been in America less than a fortnight. All of that time I spent on Father's horrid old barge, and now the barge is sunk. And as for England, I left nothing behind there worth regretting.

ANDERSEN *(Slyly)* Not even a sweetheart or two?

ANNA *(Laughing candidly)* Not even half of one.

ANDERSEN *(Jokingly)* Sure?

ANNA Positive!

ANDERSEN *(In the same joking tone)* A beautiful girl like you! I can't believe it. I think you're fibbing.

ANNA *(Flushing)* Now you're chaffing, aren't you? No, seriously, I'm glad it happened the way it did, shipwreck and everything. *(With earnest enthusiasm)* Why, I feel free for the first time in my life! It's like playing truant from my stupid old work. It's not very interesting, you know, doing the same thing over again day after day, cooped up in an office.

ANDERSEN *(Sympathetically)* I know what that means. I tried it once.

ANNA *(Smiling)* And the best part of it is that this vacation—this wonderful trip—is forced on me. I have no choice in the matter. So I can't feel guilty about not working and earning money, can I? *(She laughs)*

ANDERSEN *(Smiling)* Nope. Your guilty conscience went down with the barge.

ANNA *(Growing serious again)* And it *is* a beginning of new things for me, in a way I've just begun to know the sea—and love it! It seemed to come over me suddenly—while we were drifting in that fog with that queer silence all about. I'd always lived inland in Leeds ever since the time I was a little girl. The sea was only a name to me. And on the steamer coming over, in the steerage—that was nothing. It was only on the barge when the fog swept over us that I began to feel—it. *(She glances at his intent face, flushes, and laughs awkwardly)* You must think I'm dreadfully silly—talking this way —don't you?

ANDERSEN *(Earnestly)* Not a bit of it! It's darned interesting. And I think I know how you felt.

ANNA You mean you've felt—the same way?

ANDERSEN *(With an encouraging smile)* Tell me more about it, and I'll see.

ANNA It's so hard to put into words. *(Intensely)* As if you'd come home after being away a long, long time; as if everything suddenly had changed, and nothing could ever be the same again; as if everything you'd lived through before was small—and wrong—and could never mean anything to you again.

ANDERSEN *(Nodding slowly—his eyes wide and dreamy)* That's it. You've got it. That's the feeling exactly.

ANNA Oh, I'm so glad that someone else has had the same experience, that it's not just a silly notion of mine.

ANDERSEN *(Absent-mindedly patting her hand which is on the table beside him. She draws it away quickly, her face crimson, but one glance at his face convinces her of the innocence of this action. He speaks thoughtfully)* Foolish? Not a bit of it. It's a big, big thing—and a true thing. But why is it, I wonder? Where does it come from—for instance in your case?

ANNA *(Self-possessed again)* Perhaps it's in my blood. My father was a sailor most of his life. All the men, my father has told me, on both sides of the family have been sailors as far back as he knows about. Many of them were drowned, or died on ships and were buried at sea. *(Awed by a sudden idea)* Perhaps it is they—calling! *(Then shaking her head with a forced laugh)* But I don't believe in ghosts, do you?

ANDERSEN Sometimes when I'm on the bridge in a thick fog, I do.

ANNA *(With a nervous laugh)* Yes, that would be the time for them, wouldn't it? But when the ghosts interrupted me I was going to tell you that all the women of the family, with one exception, had married sailors. So you see—if there's anything in heredity—I must have a lot of sea concealed about me someplace.

ANDERSEN *(Thoughtfully)* Heredity might account for me, too. I've often wondered if it could be that: for my case is similar to yours—I mean, I was born and bred inland—*(With a smile)* and yet here I am.

ANNA But your family have been sailors?

ANDERSEN *(With a laugh)* Not my father! Far be it! Nor any of my brothers. Not on your life! They're all wedded to the soil. They have the greatest scorn for anyone who works on a ship.

ANNA Then, if they're that kind, why did you say—

ANDERSEN Oh, I had two uncles, my father's brothers, who went to sea. One of them died when he was captain of a steamer like this—a Swedish steamer.

ANNA *(Smiling)* I thought from your name you might be Swedish too.

ANDERSEN *(With a laugh)* Oh, but I'm not. I'm an American, born and brought up in Minnesota. My father is a Swede but an American citizen. He came over when he was a young man.

ANNA And what does he do?

ANDERSEN Farming, on a small scale. He owns a small farm and works like a slave on it—my brothers, too. It's all right for them. They like it. I tried it for a while—but it wasn't for me.

ANNA   What does your father think of your going to sea?

ANDERSEN   He makes the best of it. He knows I wasn't made for farming. He discovered that quite early—after I left high school. High school was my privilege as the youngest child. My three brothers were put to work on the farm after grammar school—and wanted to be. Well—I couldn't go the farm. I saw a chance to work my way through the university, and the farm and I parted company. Two years at college were enough. It hardly came up to my dreams. Then I bummed my way around the country for a while—as a hobo. Off and on I worked, manual labor of different kinds, but I found that slavery worse than the farm. So I drifted East and got a position with an insurance company—office work—a year of it—enough to disgust me with all indoor work for all time. I resigned on a sudden hunch and shipped away as a seaman on a tramp steamer—Australia, South Africa, the Far East—all over. Then—and then only—I began to feel the sense of finding home, you speak of. And here I am still—quite contented and unrepentant.

ANNA *(Staring at him with a fascinated astonishment)*   It's wonderful—to have lived all of that!

ANDERSEN *(With a laugh)*   Well, at any rate, I'm like you. I'm glad it all happened. It brought me—home.

ANNA   But you look so young! And this must have happened long ago.

ANDERSEN   Why? I haven't been at sea long—only a little over three years.

ANNA *(With admiration)*   And you're a second officer already!

ANDERSEN *(Laughing)*   Does that sound so hard? It isn't. It was an easy examination, and I got this berth without much trouble.

ANNA   Then it shouldn't be long before you're a captain —at that rate.

ANDERSEN *(Grinning)*   Not on your life! Never!

ANNA *(Surprised)*   But why not?

ANDERSEN   Don't want to be.

ANNA   You mean to say—   You're not serious, I know.

ANDERSEN   Yes I am—dead serious. Why should I want such a job? The skipper has the whole responsibility of the ship on his shoulders. *(Smiling)* I'm not looking for material responsibilities. I'm doing my best to avoid them.

ANNA   But—you must have changed, then. Didn't you start as a common sailor?

ANDERSEN   Yes.

ANNA   And didn't you work up to the responsible position you hold now?

ANDERSEN *(Laughing)* Responsible? A second mate? Well, perhaps, in a sense; but for me at least this job is a cinch—the easiest berth on the ship. I'm merely the captain's shadow. I toil and spin very little. The first mate has a dog's life of it—toil and trouble unending. So I don't care to be first mate any more than I do to be captain. *(With a trace of self-contempt in his mocking tones)* I'm free from the sin of ambition, you see. I'm quite content to remain where I am and let others do the aspiring. *(He laughs again rather bitterly)* It was only my laziness which made me work up so far.

ANNA Laziness?

ANDERSEN *(Amused by her bewilderment)* Exactly. The crew have to work and sweat for their pay. That was never my idea of living. I hated it, but I knew I couldn't quit—that once on the sea, I'd never be happy again away from it. I calculated carefully. I grew wise to the berth of second mate—a jewel of a position—sweatless and without a care. I resolved I'd be a second mate. So I worked like the devil for a time to fit myself to be free of hard work for all time. *(He laughs)* So you see that my laziness was the spur that goaded me on.

ANNA *(Looking at him queerly)* You're funny. I don't know now whether you aren't making fun of me.

ANDERSEN I'm not. Honor bright!

ANNA *(Frowning)* You don't look that kind.

ANDERSEN *(Taken aback)* What kind? *(He tries to laugh it off carelessly)* Oh, you mean—lazy? A waster?

ANNA   There's more to it than you've told, I know.

ANDERSEN   No. Honestly.

ANNA   But there must be something back of it. Else—
what are you doing it all for?

ANDERSEN *(Shrugging his shoulders)* What is anyone doing anything for? If one could answer that question—
*(He gets to his feet and paces back and forth. Her gaze
follows him wonderingly, full of a pity mingled with contempt. Finally he stops abruptly by her chair, throwing his
head back defiantly, his face stubborn, his eyes staring beyond her)* To live! That's the answer to your question.
That's why I'm doing it all. *(Disdainfully)* Working,
slaving, sweating to get something which only disgusts
you when you've got it! That's ambition for you! But
is it living? Not to me! Freedom—that's life! No ties,
no responsibilities—no guilty feelings. Like the sea—
always moving, never staying, never held by anything,
never giving a damn—but absorbing, taking it all in,
grabbing every opportunity to see it all—making the
world part of you and not being a grain of sand buried
and lost and held fast by other grains! Not American,
Swede—but citizen of the sea which belongs to no one.
Not love in the sense of a wife—marriage—an anchor
—but love that is free—women of all kinds and races—
Woman!

ANNA *(Who has been listening to him with fascinated eyes,
gives a startled gasp at this last)* Oh! *(Disapprovingly)*
That's stupid. It spoils all the rest.

ANDERSEN *(His outburst broken off short, stares down at her
for a moment uncomprehendingly—then with a mocking*

laugh) That last doesn't please you, eh? I suppose you're all for marriage—and stability. Naturally. *(With a quizzical smile)* But what do you think of my ambitionless ambition—as a whole?

ANNA *(Her eyes glowing)* I think it's wonderful! It's fine! It's what I feel, too.

ANDERSEN *(Astonished—half-scornfully)* What *you* feel?

ANNA *(Intensely)* What the sea has made me feel. What I felt on the barge in the fog—waiting, knowing that something was going to happen—and not caring what it was if only it led to—something different—something new.

ANDERSEN *(Looking at her with puzzled admiration)* Yes. That's it. It's strange that you— *(Quickly resuming his tone of mocking raillery)* Then you confess you're a waster, too!

ANNA Oh, no. For I don't see why you shouldn't keep on working up, become a captain, own your own ship even, and still—

ANDERSEN *(Waving this idea aside)* Responsibilities! A captain belongs to his ship first, last, and always. So does a first mate. But a second mate belongs to himself.

ANNA But if they love their ship?

ANDERSEN Then they don't love themselves enough. The sea doesn't love ships. She plays with them, destroys them, endures them because she expresses herself through them—but they belong to her, not she to them. *(While he is speaking the steward enters from the door, left forward)*

THE STEWARD   Your cabin is all ready for the young lady, sir.

ANDERSEN   All right, Steward. Thank you. *(The steward goes out. Andersen turns to Anna with a smile)* You must be worn out—by my foolish talk as much as anything.

ANNA *(Protesting excitedly)*   No. It's been wonderful. I've never heard anyone talk of those things before.

ANDERSEN *(Dismissing this with a laugh)*   And I swear I've never said those things to anyone before. One doesn't tell one's secrets to all comers. But I had to make some defence against your waster charge. And, from what you've told me of your own symptoms, I knew you'd contracted the same disease—seasickness, eh? *(He laughs mockingly—then as she doesn't reply but looks hurt by his remarks)* Shall I show you where your quarters are?

ANNA *(Getting up—matter-of-factly)*   Yes, please. *(She follows him to the doorway, left forward)*

ANDERSEN *(Pointing)*   The open door on your left where the light is. That's it. *(She nods. He smiles down into her eyes)* I won't keep you up any longer. I've got to go on watch again at four myself. I'll need a wink of sleep—if I can sleep, *now.* It's been great sport, our talk. We'll have plenty of time for more of the same—if you like.

ANNA   Yes.

ANDERSEN   You might convert me, you know.

ANNA *(With a confused laugh)*   I'm afraid you're past re-forming.

ANDERSEN   Not—by you. *(Coming nearer to her)* Well—good night.

ANNA *(Faintly)*   Good night. *(Suddenly he takes her in his arms and kisses her. She struggles fiercely and pushes him away. They stand looking at each other. She wipes her lips unconsciously with an expression of aversion, her eyes flaming at him with defiant rage and hurt. Something in her glance convinces him of his mistake. He turns away, his face growing red in his awkward shame)*

ANDERSEN *(Pleading for forbearance—in a husky voice)* You were—so beautiful—then.

ANNA *(Her voice quivering)*   You've spoiled it all. You've proved you are—what you said you were.

ANDERSEN *(With a sad laugh)*   A cad? Yes, I guess so. *(Then suddenly turning to her with impassioned entreaty)* No! Don't believe that! It wasn't I then—who did that. I knew all the time I was wrong—about you. I felt it deep down. But a mocking devil whispered that you were too good to be true. So I wanted to be convinced—   But it wasn't I—not the real myself! I swear to you it was not! Don't think of me—as that. It means so much now—your opinion—after the talk we've had—somehow. So don't—please—   I'm a rotten damn fool, I know—but not—   Say you don't believe it, won't you?

ANNA *(Deeply moved by his sincerity)* I don't want—to believe it.

ANDERSEN And you'll forgive me—and forget—that?

ANNA If you'll promise to remember—I will. *(Chris appears in the doorway, left rear. The two in the doorway, front, do not notice his coming. His eyes harden with rage and hatred as they fasten themselves on Andersen. He half crouches, his thick fingers twitching, as if he would like to spring at the second mate)*

ANDERSEN *(Very humbly)* And will you shake hands—as a token—for good night—with the real me? *(He advances his hand slowly as if fearing a refusal)*

ANNA *(With impulsive tenderness, seeing him so abject)* Of course! *(She grasps his hand)* Good night.

ANDERSEN *(Looks in her eyes for a moment)* Good night. *(He releases her hand and turns away. As he does so he sees Chris. He starts in surprise—then speaks in his mate's voice of authority)* Hello! Haven't they found you a bunk up for'ard yet?

CHRIS *(Sullenly)* Yes, Ay gat bunk—sir. *(He plainly has to force out the "sir")* Ay come for say good night to Anna.

ANDERSEN *(Repeats the name to himself half-aloud)* Anna!

ANNA The captain gave him permission, Mr. Andersen.

ANDERSEN *(Absent-mindedly)* Oh, that's all right. *(He goes out, left rear. Chris walks forward to his daughter)*

CHRIS (*Stares at her for a moment—then somberly*)   Anna! Don't go for do dat, Anna. (*His voice breaking into a pitiful pleading*) Don't go for do dat, Anna, Ay tal you!

ANNA (*With astonished bewilderment*)   What, Father? Do what?

CHRIS (*Bursting into a rage*)   Ay know! Ay see! Dat rotten fallar, he make fool of you, Anna. You look out! Ay know his kind fallar. Ay've seen many like him my time. He look pooty, he's yentleman, but he's no good sailor fallar yust same as in fo'c's'tle. You look out! He talk pooty talk, dan he gat you for marry him—

ANNA (*Staring at him as if he were mad*)   Father!

CHRIS (*Not heeding*)   He gat you for marry him, and dan you might yust s'well be dead. He go away on ship, he leave you for vait alone, he gat new gel every port. Dan you gat kits, he don't care, he don't come home, he don't know his kits even, he don't vant be bothered with kits. Oh, Ay know it's so! Your mo'der, she tal you same tang, if she's alive. She know it kill her, Ay bet you! It make you ole soon, it kill you too, Anna! (*Raising his hand as if he were taking an oath*) Ay svear, Anna, Ay vould like better you vas never been born dan you marry man dat go to sea! And Ay von't let you, no, Ay von't—no matter vat Ay gat do for stop you, py God!

ANNA (*Indignantly*)   Are you insane? What crazy talk, Father! What—as if I were dreaming of marrying anyone! How ridiculous you are!

CHRIS (*Not convinced*)   Dat ole davil, sea, she's gat us on voyage. You gat look out for her tricks now, Ay tal you!

ANNA *(With impatient scorn)*   Are you cursing the sea again? *(Defiantly)* Well, I love the sea! *(The situation suddenly strikes her as absurd, and she bends down and kisses her father laughingly)* Go to bed, you silly old goose! You're still nervous and upset or you wouldn't talk such nonsense. Get a good rest now. Good night. *(She goes out, left forward, shutting the door behind her)*

CHRIS *(Dully)*   Good night, Anna. *(He stands still for a moment, brooding somberly. Then he shakes his fist at the sea outside with a hopeless rage)* Damn ole davil! *(He turns, his shoulders bowed wearily, and plods toward the doorway, left rear*

as

(The Curtain Falls)

Scene—About a month later—The seamen's section of the forecastle on the Londonderry, *at anchor in the roadstead, Buenos Aires. The forecastle is a small, low, triangular-shaped compartment with tiers of bunks, three deep, built in along the sides. It narrows to an apex at the far end (toward the bow of the ship). The left wall, with its rows of bunks, runs straight back, following the line of the alleyway outside which separates the seamen's from the firemen's quarters. The bunks on the right follow the line of the ship's hull curving in at the bow. Several portholes are seen over the upper tier on this side. Low, wooden benches border the edge of the constricted floor space. Blankets lie in heaps as they were tossed aside in most of the bunks. On the left, forward, a doorway opening on the alleyway leading to the main deck. To the rear of the door top, a lighted lamp stands in a bracket fastened to the wall.*

It is about nine o'clock at night.

As the curtain rises, Chris, Jonesy, and Edwards are discovered. Chris is lying on his side in a lower bunk on the right, his head propped on his hand. He stares moodily before him, evidently deep in somber thought. Jonesy is seated on a bench on the left near the doorway, as close to the light as he can get. He is a stout, heavy-faced, good-natured-looking young fellow. His sleeves are rolled up to the elbows; he has a battered suitcase on his knees serving as desk; he is writing a letter, his brow furrowed by the effort at concentration, his thick, red fingers clenched about the pencil as if it were a chisel. He makes the letters with difficulty, with painstaking slowness, sticking out his tongue as he completes each sentence. Edwards, a tall, lanky, dark-complected boy of eighteen, sits by his side, bent forward, smoking a pipe, watching his mate's efforts impatiently with a scornful amusement. All are dressed in dungarees, flannel shirts, etc.

EDWARDS *(Impatiently)* Aw, chuck the bloody letter, Jonesy. Finish it some other time. It's hot 's hell in here. Let's get out on deck. The moon's up. All the rest is out there.

JONESY *(Without looking up)* Must be all dead. I don't 'ear no talkin'.

EDWARDS That's count o' the bo'sun. He's bad tonight, they says—fever and stuff—and the skipper sends orders to douse the noise. They're takin' the bos to the hospital first thing in the mornin', I heard. The rheumatics has him done for.

JONESY *(Unfeelingly)* Serve 'im bloody right—the slave-drivin' image!

EDWARDS He'll not be with us next trip, that's safe. We'll be signin' on another bo'sun. *(Nudging Jonesy with his elbow—with a grin)* Maybe skipper'll give ole Chris the job. He useter to bo'sun, he says. *(Jonesy looks up with a chuckle)*

CHRIS *(Surlily)* Ay don't take yob on dis scow dey give me hundred dollar a day.

EDWARDS *(Imitating Chris' accent)* Dat's fallar, py golly! *(He and Jonesy roar with laughter. Chris grunts angrily)*

JONESY *(Bending to his writing again)* Hush your jaw, Eds. Don't you see I'm tryin' to think? I can't when you're blatherin'. *(He finishes a sentence and looks up)* I got to finish the damn thing now I'm started—or I never will.

EDWARDS *(Disgustedly)* What's the good of it? What's there to write about? Nothin' never happens on this old hooker.

JONESY That's what bloody well makes it 'ard on a bloke. I got to make it up out o' me own 'ead.

EDWARDS Then chuck it!

JONESY No. I ain't written the old woman a line in a year a'most. She'll think I'm gone to Davy Jones. No, blarst it, I'm at it, and I'll finish, and then the rotten thing'll be off my mind. *(With exasperation)* But what in 'ell can yer write your mother about? Yer can't tell 'er what 'appened in port, can yer? You can't say: "Dear Ma, when I was in Boston I was as drunk as drunk and spent all my money." Ho! That'd set 'er cursin' and blindin' 'er old 'ead off! And, same's you said, nothin' never 'appens on this tub to write about. *(He grips his pencil again savagely)* But I'm goin' to finish the blarsted thing, Gawd blind it!

EDWARDS You're off your chump! *(He turns and regards Chris curiously for a moment)* What's up with you, old Chris? Feelin' off your oats?

CHRIS *(Glumly)* No. Ay'm all right.

EDWARDS   You'd never think it, lookin' at you. You're a funny bloke. Ain't you glad the voyage is over? I'd be dancin' out on deck if I was in your boots. You'll go ashore tomorrer in Bonos Ares and be your own boss again. And the skipper'll give you a month's pay, I'll bet. He's a soft old bird like that. You'll be able to have a bloody good drunk 'fore the consul ships you back to the States.

CHRIS *(Angrily)*   Ay don't vant for go on drunk any more, Ay tal you!

EDWARDS *(With a chuckle)*   Oh, I was forgettin' your girl was on board. She'd give you hell if you did, eh?

CHRIS *(Irritably)*   Dat ain't none of your business.

JONESY *(Looking up—with a grin)*   'Is gel? She won't be 'is gel long, you can take my word for it.

CHRIS *(Glancing at him with dark suspicion)*   Vat you mean, Yonesy?

JONESY *(Derisively)*   Don't arsk me. Arsk the second mate.

CHRIS *(Furiously—half scrambling out of his bunk)*   You mind your own damn business, you fallar!

JONESY *(Grinning)*   You ain't gettin' mad at me, are yer? No 'arm meant, ole Chris, s'elp me! I was on'y sayin' what all of us 'as seen with our two eyes. 'E's dead gone on 'er, the second, it's plain 's the nose on yer face. *(Placatingly, as Chris continues to glare at him)* I didn't mean nothin' bad, ole Chris, s'elp me. 'Is missis, reg'lar married is what I meant.

CHRIS *(Furiously)* Shut up, you damn liar, you! *(He springs out of his bunk threateningly)*

JONESY *(As Edwards roars with laughter—provokingly)* You do take it to 'eart, don't yer? What's the trouble? Don't yer like Andersen?

EDWARDS *(With sudden scorn)* Aw, he's a crazy Dutchy. A second mate ain't good enough for his girl, I s'pose. Wants a skipper—or the King of England. And him takin' his watch on deck with the rest of us!

CHRIS *(His anger passing away)* Ay'm big fool for gat angry. You is yust young boys. You don't know. Ay don't vant King of England for Anna, Ay don't vant no man. Ay vant her for mysalf. She's all Ay gat in vorld. *(He sits down on a bench dejectedly. The two boys are a bit shame-faced and remain silent, Jonesy pretending to write again)*

EDWARDS *(Getting to his feet)* Well, I wisht I was in your boots just the same—gettin' paid off tomorrer. How'd you like to be me, eh?—signed on for a year more on this lousy lime-juicer. *(He grunts—then stretches lazily)* You won't chuck the writin' and come out on deck, Jonesy?

JONESY No. I'll be finished in 'arf a mo.

EDWARDS I'll sling my hook, then. It'd choke you in here. *(He saunters out. There is a pause. Jonesy scowls and sweats over his letter)*

CHRIS *(Kindly)*   You write your mo'der, Yonesy?

JONESY   Yes.

CHRIS *(Approvingly)*   Dat's good boy. Don't let dat fallar Ed stop you from write. Your mo'der, she vorry like thunder, she tank maybe you're drowned, you don't write.

JONESY *(Looking up—with cynical amusement)*   Worry? Not 'er! She ain't got time. There's 'leven of us boys and gels she's got. If she was to start worryin' over each of us, she'd go balmy quick. Ho, no! She ain't worrin'. But I might 's well let 'er know I'm live and kickin'. *(He starts in writing)* She ain't a bad one, the ole woman—'less she's got a cargo of gin aboard. *(As he finishes speaking, Glass, the messroom steward, comes into the forecastle. He is a slight, dark young fellow of twenty-five or so. His thin face with its long pointed nose; its large mouth twisted to one side, the upper lip shadowed by a wisp of mustache; its sharp, mocking, pale blue eyes; has the expression of half-cruel, malicious humor which character-izes the practical joker. He wears a short, white jacket, white duck pants, and sneakers—all passably clean)*

GLASS *(Breezily)*   What ho, Jonesy, me lad. *(His eyes fix themselves immediately on Chris with the eager satisfaction of one who has found his victim. He grins)* And hello, if here ain't old Chris, old scuttle!

CHRIS *(With a grunt of dislike)*   Vell, vat about ole Chris? You try make fun, you fallar?

GLASS *(With feigned indignation)*   Can't I say a civil word to you without you gettin' on your ear? Do you think

I'm always jokin'? I never seed the like of the mob on this kettle. They don't believe a word a man says. *(He catches Jonesy's eye and winks at him slyly. Jonesy, anticipating fun from this signal, puts his suitcase and letter on the bench beside him and leans back against the bunks with an expectant smirk)*

CHRIS *(A bit mollified)*   You don't act like crazy fool, ve believe you.

GLASS *(Sitting down opposite Chris)*   Well, I'm not acting like a fool now, am I? If you think I am, say so, and I'll get out of this. There ain't no use tryin' to tell things to a man that won't believe you.

CHRIS *(Suspiciously)*   You vant tal *me* sometang?

GLASS   That's what I came here for. You don't s'pose, when it's cool and moonlight on deck so clear you'd read a book by it, that I'd be comin' to this sweet room for pleasure do you? No, I was lookin' you up to have a talk with you as man to man. You can believe or not. Just the same, I'm dead serious, old Chris.

CHRIS *(Looking at him doubtfully)*   Vat you gat for tal me, Glass?

GLASS   A lot o' things you've a right to know.

CHRIS *(His curiosity aroused)*   Vat tangs?

GLASS *(Staring upward—carelessly)*   About two people— on this boat.

CHRIS *(Frowning)* Vat two people?

GLASS One is an officer.

CHRIS *(Savagely)* Hmmph!

GLASS The other's a passenger.

CHRIS *(Springing to his feet and shaking his fist in Glass' face)* Shut up, you! Don't make no lying yoke with me, you fool fallar! Ay break your face, you do!

GLASS *(Rising with an air of hurt dignity)* Did you ever see the beat of him, Jonesy? *(Turning to Chris with well-feigned anger)* All right, you goat-nose Swede, if that's the way you feel about it! No one's forcin' you to lissen, is there? That's the thanks I get for tryin' to do a good turn for you. Well, you can go to hell now, for all of me. Keep on bein' as blind as a bat and have the whole world laughin' at you—till it's too late. All I was goin' to do was to tell you somethin' that'd maybe open your eyes, and put some sense in your thick, square head—and make you show if you was a sheep or had the guts of a man. *(He takes a few steps toward the door)* You're scared to learn the truth, that's what. You're a sheep.

CHRIS *(Stares at his back for a moment undecidedly, then sits down again—with angry contempt)* Ay'm not scared any man on dis ship, py golly! Ay break you in half with little finger, you skinny grasshopper!

GLASS *(Pretending to ignore this—with a wink at Jonesy— pleasantly)* Writin' a letter to your girl, Jonesy?

JONESY *(Grinning back at him)*   No—the ole woman.

CHRIS *(In a loud tone of scorn which nevertheless reveals a troubled curiosity)*   Fallars on dis ship make anyone sick! Yust talk, talk—tangs dey don't know nutting about—yust like pack of ole vomen round stove!

GLASS *(Keeping his back turned but raising his voice—with elaborate sarcasm)*   Of course, *I* couldn't know nothin' 'bout *them*. *I'm* on'y up on the bridge deck, where *they* are, most of the time. So you couldn't expect *me* to know nothin', or *see* nothin', or *hear* nothin', could you, Jonesy?

JONESY   Ho! You sees a lot ole Chris don't see, I'll lay my oath!

CHRIS *(This shaft has bitten deep but he growls)*   He don't see nutting, dat fallar. He make up lies. *(As Glass makes no reply, he is forced to address him directly—scornfully)* Vat you *tank* you see, Glass?

GLASS *(Turning to him—stiffly)*   Nothin'—as if I'd tell you any more, old Dutchy.

CHRIS *(After a pause—insinuatingly)*   Ay tank you make fun. Dat make me angry. You alvays make fun, you know dat, Glass. If Ay tank you talk straight and don't lie—

GLASS   And be insulted again for my pains, eh? Not much!

CHRIS   Ay'm not angry no more. *(Questioningly)* Ay'm sure you don't make fun dis time, Glass?

GLASS *(Very earnestly)* I won't deny I like my joke—in most things. But when it comes to talkin' as man to man with a man—about serious things, mind!—you'll find I'm the last one in the world to laugh. *(He turns to Jonesy with a wink)* You can ask Jonesy. He's known me a while and he'll tell you. Ain't that right, Jonesy?

JONESY *(Concealing his grin—heartily)* Right as rain!

CHRIS *(Persuasively)* Sat down, dan. You tal me—*(With an attempt to belittle the matter)*—all dem big tangs, eh?

GLASS *(Pretending reluctance)* You'll promise you'll not get on your high horse at anythin'—the truth, man!—I tells you?

CHRIS Yes. Ay'm cool as cucumber now. *(Forcing a grin)* You ain't gat nothin' for tal, Ay bet you.

GLASS Oho, ain't I! *(He sits down and leans over to Chris confidentially)* I won't beat about the bush. I'll come straight to the point to prove I'm not foolin'. I'll tell you straight out, if I was you, I'd not trust any girl of mine with that second mate.

CHRIS *(His face darkening—tries to force a careless laugh)* Is dat all you gat tal? You don't know. Anna's strong gel. She know how for take care of hersalf, py yingo!

GLASS *(With provoking scorn)* You like the second, I'll bet, in spite of all your talk.

CHRIS *(Violently)* Like? Ay hate dat fallar! He's no good for no one.

GLASS *(Eagerly, seeing that he now has his victim where he wants him)* No good? You ain't tellin' no lie, old Chris! He ain't no good, that's a fact. You must've heard something about him, ain't you?

CHRIS No, Ay hear tangs about him, but Ay don't care for dat. Ay can tal dem kind fallar ven Ay see him, vithout Ay hear nutting.

GLASS *(Thoughtfully)* Man, I could tell you a few things that'd make you prick up your ears.

CHRIS *(Scowling)* Vat tangs you mean?

GLASS I'm not findin' fault with his doin's on my own account, mind! The second's a good sport from his toes up—a man as ain't afraid to go on a bloody drunk when he's a mind to, and don't care who knows it. And the girls—they all go crazy after him, man! He's left them broken-hearted after him in every port we've touched since he's been aboard—and he goes laughin' on to the next one. What's a girl more or less to him? He's that big and handsome, there's not one of the lot wouldn't leave home and mother if he crooked his little finger.

CHRIS *(Savagely)* It's so, Ay guess. *(Suspiciously)* But how you come for know all dem tangs, Glass?

GLASS *(In scornful amazement)* Know them? Do you think I'm tellin' you a secret? Every blarsted man on board the *Londonderry* could tell you the same thing. Couldn't they, Jonesy?

JONESY *(Concealing a snicker)* Aye.

GLASS   He's not the one to hide what he's doin', the second. He's proud of it, s'help me! Why, last time we was here in Buenos Aires I went to the Casino to see the wrestling match—and there was Andersen in a box, as drunk as a lord, with a big, blond girl—a beauty, man!—sittin' on his lap. They was kissin' each other, not givin' a damn for no one, and the whole crowd in the place watchin' 'em and laughin'.

CHRIS   *(Clenching his fists and growling)*   Dirty svine!

GLASS   *(With a grin over his shoulder at Jonesy)*   Oh, he ain't so bad—as a man with men. He spends his pay day like a sport and a sailor. No savin' money, no stinginess about him. He worked up from the fo'c's'tle, he did. He wasn't no lady-boy apprentice, ever. So he's a good sport and a real seaman of the old school—like you, old Chris.

CHRIS   *(With hatred)*   Dat's vorst tang he can be, Ay tank. Dat's damn fool business. Dat's dat ole davil sea's dirty tricks. *(He shakes his fist—then with bewilderment)* You're crazy fallar, Glass. One minute you say he's no good, next minute say he is good. Vat you talkin' about, eh?

GLASS   Lissen! I say he's a sport after my own heart, and I like him well enough myself even if he is a Yank—*but*—I ain't got no young daughter that's a nice girl, don't forget!

CHRIS   *(Glumly)*   Anna look out for hersalf, Ay tal you!

GLASS   *(Indignantly)*   That's a sweet way for you to talk! Are you her father, or ain't you? Ain't you bound to look after her when her mother's dead? It's your fault, her gettin' aboard, ain't it? Look out for herself? There's lots he's left behind that thought— Well, if you don't care that much, I s'pose there's no good talkin'. But remember that I did my best to give you a hand.

CHRIS *(Trying to reassure himself)* Oh, you Glass, you make all tangs bigger. It's all right. Ve're in port now, ve go ashore in morning, she don't see him again. *(Spitting disgustedly)* She don't care for fool fallar dat go on sea, anyvay. She's gat too much sense for dat.

GLASS *(Mockingly)* She don't, eh? Lissen to him, Jonesy! Just lissen to him!

JONESY 'E's a silly bird.

CHRIS *(Vehemently)* Ay tal you it's so. She make fun, dat's all.

GLASS Fun! Lissen to him! If you'd seen what I seed last night—

CHRIS Vat? *(Threateningly)* Don't you go for lie now, you hear?

GLASS Did I say it was anythin' wrong? Don't I know your Anna ain't that kind? Can't I tell by the looks of her? It ain't nothin' not right I'm speakin' of; but Ed was tellin' me you don't even want her to marry him.

CHRIS *(Savagely)* No! Anna marry dat drunk, no good, sailor fallar? Ay svear Ay kill him first!

GLASS *(With an air of decision—calmly)*   Then you lose, Chris, old love.

CHRIS *(Perplexed)*   Eh?

GLASS   You lose, I said.

CHRIS   Ay lose? Vat Ay lose?

GLASS   Her! *(With a grin)* You better get out your old pistol and shoot him. You ain't got so much time, either. They'll both be ashore tomorrow.

CHRIS *(Menacingly)*   Yes—but Ay-Ay vill be ashore, too.

GLASS   Oh, they'll give you the slip—after you're good and drunk.

CHRIS *(Angrily)*   Ay don't gat drunk no more, Ay tal you!

GLASS   Many a man's sworn the same and woke up in jail next mornin' with a drunk and disorderly against him. *(Tormentingly)* They'll be man and wife when they come to bail you out. *(Jonesy laughs)*

CHRIS *(Starting to his feet—furiously)*   Shut up, you big fool! All you talk is crazy tangs. Anna don't care nutting, vouldn't marry dat fallar, he gat million dollar. You make joke, ain't it so?

GLASS *(Carelessly)*   If it's a joke, it's one on you. You wouldn't call it a joke if you seen 'em last night.

CHRIS (*In rage and misery*)   You don't see dem. You're liar, dat's vat!

GLASS   I was going up the starb'rd ladder to the bridge deck when I seen 'em—'bout six bells, it was. I stopped when I heard the voices and bent down in the shadow, listenin'. Says I to myself: Here's where I can do a good turn for old Chris, likely. They'll maybe be sayin' somethin' as he had ought to know about. They didn't heed me comin'. They was too busy with themselves. And it was that still and calm, if you remember, I could hear every word. Andersen was tellin' your girl how much he loved and all that stuff. It took him a long time to get to the point but in the end he says: "Will you marry me?" And she waits a bit and then answers: "Yes," says she.

CHRIS (*Raging, grabs Glass by the shoulders and shakes him furiously*)   Anna don't say dat! Dat's lie, Ay tal you!

GLASS (*Writhing in his grip*)   On my oath! Believe it or not. (*Whining with pain*) Leggo me, Dutchy, blarst you! (*Chris seems to come to himself. He takes his hands away and drops down on a bench, staring before him with beaten, wounded eyes, his spirit broken, his shoulders sagging wearily. Glass moves his sore shoulders and glares at him resentfully*) That's what I get for tryin' to beat some brains into your square head, is it? (*Viciously*) Well, I hope the second does make a bleedin' fool of you, that's what!

CHRIS (*Gets up distractedly as if he couldn't bear to listen to the other's voice a second longer*)   Shut up! Shut up! Ay gat go out on deck vere I don't hear you. (*He goes out*)

GLASS *(Shouting after him)* Take a jump over the side and drown ye'self for all I cares! *(He turns to Jonesy grumblingly)* He near broke my shoulders, the fathead Swede! Arms on him like a hairy gorilla, he has.

JONESY *(Chuckling)* You didn't 'arf 'ave 'im on a string. 'E swallowed it all, 'ook, line and sinker. And did yer look at 'im? 'E's mad as a bloody 'ornet at the second. *(He laughs gleefully)* Blimey, but 'e'll kick up a bloody row with 'im, wait 'n' see!

GLASS *(Grinning)* And the second won't dare beat him, 'count of the girl.

JONESY *(Still more tickled)* Ho-ho! You're a foxey joker, Glass. If you'd seed the serious face on you when you was tellin' it. I was almost taken in by it myself. Was any of it truth?

GLASS *(With a chuckle)* Sure—a good bit of it—on'y not the way I told it, exactly. You know right enough what I said about the second is Gospel. He does spend his money like a sport, and he does go on sprees, and he does fool with the girls. *(He grins)* But what I told of the blond girl sittin' on his lap in the Casino and kissin' him—I made that up out of my head.

JONESY Ho-ho! Blimey!

GLASS Still, why ain't it true? He's the kind to do it. It might have happened just 's well 's not.

JONESY And that about him askin' Chris' gel to marry 'im?

GLASS *(Candidly)* That's Gawd's truth, Jonesy! And I was there listenin' to hear what I could hear, like I says. *(He grins)* But the end of it wasn't hardly what I told him.

JONESY *(Excitedly)* It wasn't? What'd they do, then?

GLASS She didn't say yes, Chris' girl didn't. She said no. *(As Jonesy stares at him with astonished doubt, he continues impressively)* She doesn't speak for a long time, keepin' him waitin' while she's lookin' out over the water—then "no," she says—and you could tell she meant it, too—very low but clear so's I heard it plain as you hear me now.

JONESY *(The humor of the situation suddenly striking him)* And you told ole Chris—Gawd's truth!—but you've made a bloody mess of it! The second'll bash 'is 'ead in! Blimey! Ho-ho!

GLASS Serve him right! Someone had ought to bust his face in. Silly fathead! Him talkin' 'bout not lettin' his girl marry a sailor, or anyone'd go to sea, not even a bloody officer! He's a fine one to talk—deck hand on a rotten coal barge! Who does he think he is, I wonder —a squarehead furriner! He'd ought to be glad the second'd look at his girl, and mean decent. And her! She seems nice enough; but puttin' on airs, talkin' like a bloody lady! If it wasn't for her looks she'd be scrubbin' floors. She'd ought to get down on her knees to nab a man like the second, with officer's pay.

JONESY Maybe she's 'eard of 'is foolin' with other gels. Maybe she's got another bloke in the States. *(Philosoph-*

ically) Gels is funny blokes. *(Good-naturedly)* And ole Chris is all right—a good mate in the fo'c's'tle and a smart sailor—bo'sun, 'e was once—on'y 'e's a bit off 'is 'ead. *(Laughing)* Ho-ho! There'll be some bloody fun on this bloody hooker in the mornin' if ole Chris gets started! You'd better lie low till 'e gets ashore, Glass. If 'e finds out you was lyin' to 'im, it won't be 'ealthy for you to meet 'im.

GLASS *(With a smile)* I'll get the fourth engineer to sneak me in his cabin if there's any trouble. *(Yawning)* Well, it'll give the Swede somethin' to think about for one night, anyway. He won't sleep much, I'll bet. I wonder why he's so down on sailors.

JONESY 'E don't seem to be with us 'ere. It's on'y with 'is gel, 'e means.

GLASS He's off his chump, like you says, must be. *(Stretching)* I'm for out on deck. Goin' to finish your letter?

JONESY *(Taking suitcase, paper and pencil again—obstinately)* Yes, blarst it!

GLASS I'll pop off. *(He saunters out. Jonesy, scowling fiercely, bends to his labors. A moment later Chris reenters and sits down again. Jonesy looks up, then goes on writing. Chris broods somberly)*

CHRIS *(After a pause—with a grim determination—aloud to himself)* Only one tang left for do, py yingo! *(Jonesy looks up. Chris takes his sheath knife from his belt and holds it in his hands, regarding it with a morbid fascination)*

Only one vay for save Anna from dat ole davil. Eh—
oh—it's so!

JONESY *(Jeeringly)*   What ole devil? The second?

CHRIS   Eh, him? He don't count, dat fool fallar. He don't
count for himself. But he's sailor—yust like Ay vas
once—he's no good—he belong to sea—he's one of her
dirty tricks.

JONESY *(With a guffaw)*   'Er? Your gel?

CHRIS   No—ole davil, sea.

JONESY   The sea? What in 'ell are yer talkin' 'bout? *(Contemptuously)* Blimey! You're a balmy ole bird!

CHRIS *(Not heeding this—in the same strange, determined
way as if he were giving speech to something he had worked
out carefully in his own mind)*   Ay gat do it. Ay beat
dat ole davil yet, py yimminy! She don't gat Anna like
her mo'der, no, Ay svear! And Anna forgat in time.
Forgat him, forgat me. She hate sea like hell after—dis
—happen. *(He nods his head)* It's only tang, yes. Ay
can't help it.

JONESY *(Irritably)*   Hush your bleedin' gab! 'Ow the 'ell
can I write when you're ravin' like a lunatic?

CHRIS *(Fingering the edge of the knife—dully)*   You ain't
gat stone for sharpen knife, Yonesy?

JONESY   No. Shut yer marf! Chips 'as got one.

CHRIS Ay got gat him. It's dull—dis knife. *(He goes out slowly)*

JONESY *(Stares after him for a second, seized with a vague foreboding. Then he shakes this off irritably)* Ho, t'ell with 'im! *He starts writing again*
as

(The Curtain Falls)

Act Three—Scene 2

Scene—A section of the midship of the Londonderry, *looking astern. In the foreground, a short stretch of the main deck about ten feet deep from front to rear. On both sides of this, fencing it in, are the steel bulwarks of the ship, about three and a half feet high. In the rear, the bridge deck rises eight feet above the main. It is reached by two steel ladders, placed port and starboard. On the bridge deck, allowing a free deck space of about six feet on each side, stands the cabin with its row of brass-rimmed portholes. It sets back a little from the front edge of the bridge deck, allowing a narrow space in front of it, shut in by a steel rail, along which one can walk in passing from port to starboard. Over the cabin, extending the full width of the ship, is the bridge itself, a glimpse of which can be seen with its canvas awning, its wheel house and chart room in the center, its deck, rail high, fenced in by taut, canvas strips.*

All of this superstructure of the ship is painted white. The rest—bulwarks, main deck, everything below the bridge deck is painted black.

Bright, intense moonlight falls full on the ship. The shadows stretch astern. Every object stands plainly revealed. The vessel rides, motionless, on the calm waters of the roadstand. Silence and moonlight brood as one spirit over the ship. It is evidently late, for there is no sound of any human activity. The row of portholes toward the center of the cabin are alight, however, showing there is still someone awake. Their bright, yellow light sheds forth in golden strips, then filters into the lucent moon-grey and is lost. Over the bulwarks a vista of still-flowing river, spattered with silver rain, can be seen, a black line of low-lying land marking the horizon. The sky is wan and withdrawn, faintly glimmering with stars.

As the curtain rises, there is silence for a moment. Then a slight noise, like the shuffling of a foot, is heard from the left where the bulwark curves upward to the bridge deck. There is a black patch of shadow there between the ladder and the bulwark. The figure of Chris can be dimly made out, crouching on his haunches, his body pressed into the angle to avoid discovery from above. His head is tilted back; his eyes stare up at the bridge deck; he listens intently for some sound of movement from that direction.

His watch is rewarded. A door on the left of the cabin is opened and Andersen comes out. For a moment he stands in the block of thin yellow light from the open door; then he closes it behind him. Chris starts and half straightens his bent body. Andersen goes to the rail on the left of the bridge deck and stands there for a second. He sighs heavily, his eyes staring out over the water. Then he shakes his head doggedly as if to get rid of his thoughts, and clears his throat impatiently. Chris stiffens into an attitude of threatening vigilance. He has recognized the voice. Andersen takes out his watch and peers at it in the moonlight. Then, putting it back, he walks slowly around the corner of the cabin to the strip of railed-in deck in front of the portholes. He walks across toward the right. As he does so, Chris slinks quickly from his hiding place and bounds up the ladder, his bare feet making no noise on the steel rungs. Gaining the deck above, he crouches against the left wall of the cabin in the shadow falling from the bridge overhead. Andersen stops as he nears the end of the cabin on the right and, leaning against the rail, his face turned toward the right, he remains as if waiting for someone. Chris moves forward silently out of the shadow and peers around the corner of the cabin. He has a knife clutched in his right hand. He sees that the second mate's back is toward him, and, bending low so as to be beneath the sweep of the lighted portholes, he advances noiselessly three slow, careful steps. Then he gathers himself together and seems to be about to make a rushing spring at Andersen when the silence is shattered by the ship's bell which tolls with a mellow booming six times. Panic-stricken by this unforeseen interruption, Chris turns tail and darts back around the corner to his hiding place in the shadow of the bridge. Andersen stands motionless until the sound of the bell dies away. Then a door is opened on the right of the cabin and Anna comes out. Andersen hears this and strides forward eagerly around the corner of the cabin to meet her. He takes her hand without speaking. She withdraws it quickly.

ANDERSEN *(In a low voice)* Out there in front of the cabin. The moonlight's beautiful there. *(He motions her to precede him)*

ANNA *(Walking before the portholes and looking out over the sea—raptly)* It's beautiful everywhere tonight. What a night! It's like living in a dream. *(She has stopped at the center of the strip of deck)*

ANDERSEN Let's go further on. The skipper's still up, you know, going over his papers, and if he heard us talking he'd probably come out and join in. We don't want any number three—tonight.

ANNA *(Walking along almost to the end of the cabin on left —uncertainly)* It might be better—if—

ANDERSEN *(Fiercely)* No, no, Anna! Not our last night together!

ANNA *(Sadly)* This *is* the end, isn't it? Tomorrow I'll have to say good'bye to this dear old ship.

ANDERSEN *(In a tone of pain)* Don't, Anna. Don't speak of it.

ANNA *(As if she had not heard him)* And then I suppose it'll be steerage passage back to the States for me and Father—and then a beginning of the old, dull life all over again. *(She sighs. Chris slinks out of the shadow of the bridge and cautiously peers around the corner. They are side by side, their faces turned toward the bow, and they cannot see him. Chris discovers that his daughter is now between him and Andersen. He draws his head back quickly, his face working with baffled fury. He cannot escape toward the forecastle now; he is afraid to move; he is forced to remain an eavesdropper. Besides, he is consumed by curiosity. He leans against the side of the cabin, his head cocked to one side, trying to hear every word that passes between them)*

ANDERSEN *(Eagerly)* You don't have to go back to the old life, Anna. *(Pleadingly)* If you'd only—

ANNA *(Shrinking away from him—in a frightened tone)* Please! You promised you'd not speak of that again— or I'd not have come tonight. *(He groans helplessly. There is an uncomfortable pause—then she goes on sadly)* When I was inside waiting for six bells to strike, I got to thinking of things. I tried to argue sensibly with myself and make myself become at least as hopeful about the future as I used to be in England. I tried to feel assured that I'd be contented again with my old plans and dreams. *(She gives an unhappy laugh)* But they seemed too dreadful—and stupid—and such a waste of life.

ANDERSEN Then why go back to them, Anna?

ANNA *(Ignoring this question)* This trip has been too splendid. It's spoiled me for commonplace things, I'm afraid. The sea has made me discover so many feelings I never knew I had before. *(She laughs unhappily)* Perhaps it's only my natural laziness sprouting out, but the way I feel now I'd be happy—oh, so happy!—just forever sailing here and there, watching the sun rise and sink into the sea again day after day—and never do anything but love the sea.

ANDERSEN *(Impatiently)* You could do all that if you'd only—

ANNA *(Putting her hands over her ears—frightenedly)* Ssshh! Please!

ANDERSEN *(With a helpless groan)* Oh—the devil take promises!

ANNA *(After a pause—rebelliously)* I don't want to go back to any life I've ever lived before—but what else can I do?

ANDERSEN Are you asking me? *(With a bitter smile)* I made a suggestion last night.

ANNA Don't. We're talking of things that are—possible. And you're not trying to help me.

ANDERSEN I tried to help us both, but—

ANNA *(Shortly)* Please!

ANDERSEN *(Offended—sarcastically)* Well then, when your father becomes captain, mate and crew of an-

other barge, you might sign on as general house-
keeper.

ANNA *(Hurt—coldly)*   It's serious with me. *(After a pause she continues slowly)* No, I'm afraid Father and I will have to separate. *(Chris gives a start as he hears this. His face winces as if he had been struck)* I don't think I have a good effect on him, or he on me. In the first days, after I grew to know him on the barge, I was happy because I thought I had found a real father I could love and respect. He was so kind and gentle—and different— and he worked so hard and uncomplainingly, and he seemed so happy to have me with him. I thought I had at last found something real to work for—to give him a home, a real home, in his old age. *(She sighs. Chris makes a movement as if he wanted to hide himself in the shadow again)* But since the fog—since we've been on the steamer—he's changed, and he seems a stranger to me now more than ever. We've hardly spoken to each other in the last two weeks. He glares at me as if he hated me. And when he does speak he says such strange things—over and over—that silly idea I've told you of about the sea—the old devil, he calls her—that will swallow me up. *(With a shudder of fear)* It's silly—but I'm growing afraid of him—and of what he says. It sinks in. It gets on my nerves until I'm in terror of the sea myself. *(She points out and smiles raptly)* Imagine being afraid of anything so lovely!

ANDERSEN *(Frowning)*   He hates to see me with you. That's it.

ANNA   No, I really believe this enforced trip to sea again has affected his mind. He's so queer.

ANDERSEN *(Contemptuously)*   Queer? We're all queer. Your father's brand of queerness is common enough, only he's got enough of the old sea superstitions in his blood to make him believe in his ghosts. But I tell you what: It's fear, that's what's the matter with him. He's afraid. He swallowed the anchor, as the sailors say. *(Chris half opens his mouth as if he were going to shout an indignant denial of this charge)*

ANNA *(Curiously)*   What a funny expression. What does it mean?

ANDERSEN   To swallow the anchor? It means just this: To loose your grip, to whine and blame something outside of yourself for your misfortunes, to quit and refuse to fight back any more, to be afraid to take any more chances because you're sure you're no longer strong enough to make things come out right, to shrink from any more effort and be content to anchor fast in the thing you are!

ANNA *(Looking at him with wonder)*   It's strange to hear you talk that way—with your ideas of things.

ANDERSEN *(Bitterly)*   Oh, you're not the only one who has changed since you came on board—though you probably haven't been interested enough to see it. But we'll let that pass. I was telling you that your father had swallowed the anchor. The sea was his life, wasn't it? And now he blames it for all that happened to him, and hates and fears it accordingly. It's life he's really afraid of, if he only knew it—his own life.

ANNA *(Kindly)*   I suppose that is it. Poor Father!

ANDERSEN   He has an excuse—if there ever is any. He's an old man. Oh, I'm not blaming him. I've hardly the right to. We've all of us done the same thing at times —swallowed the anchor!

ANNA *(Astonished)*   Why do you talk so bitterly?

ANDERSEN *(With a laugh)*   Why not? Who has a better right? For I know the game. I swallowed the anchor the day I became second mate.

ANNA *(Rising to his defense)*   That's not true. You wanted to live differently—to see the world.

ANDERSEN   That was my sugar-coated illusion. But the truth is that I wanted to enjoy everything and go scot free of payment. I want to sponge, to let someone else pay. It's a good enough idea, if you're small enough for it, though I don't doubt that you'd be forced to pay tenfold in the end—when you were old. Yes, I was small enough for it—then. I'm not now. I can see— bigger things. *(She turns away her head to hide the fact that she is moved by his talk. He goes on bitterly again)* And you—oh, yes, you've swallowed the anchor, too! You're afraid to go on, afraid to be yourself. You whine: "what else can I do?" You're stuck fast. You'll go back to the old things.

ANNA *(Her face flushing—turning on him indignantly)* What are you saying? Please don't meddle—   *(But she drops her eyes before his—in a trembling voice)* You're insulting.

ANDERSEN   You know it's true, Anna. *(She turns away. There is a pause. He goes on bitterly)* And I? I had just

135

heaved my anchor up on deck again, and got my ship refitted for sea. It wasn't such an easy job as you might think. And now there's no port to sail to! So it's over-board—down my throat—it'll have to go again, once and for all time.

ANNA *(Instinctively putting her hand on his arm—plead-ingly)* Don't. It hurts me to hear you talk that way.

ANDERSEN *(Taking her hand in both of his)* Then why won't you—why won't you marry me, Anna? *(Chris stands up straight at this, an expression of amazed joy coming over his face as he knows that Glass' story must have been a lie. Anna opens her lips to voice a frightened protest but Andersen interrupts her fiercely)* Oh, I know I promised not to speak of it again—after last night. But how can I help it? What else in God's world can I talk about? What else matters? What is my life now but you?

ANNA *(Struggling to free her hands—weakly)* Don't. I'm going—in.

ANDERSEN Not till we've thrashed this thing out, you're not! No, not if I have to tie you here. *(Chris raises the knife in his hand and seems about to spring around the corner of the cabin)*

ANNA *(Pleading—weakly)* But it's no good—it will only hurt us, Paul—it's better—as it is.

ANDERSEN *(Insistently)* Hurt *us*? But that means—it hurts you too, Anna. And if you don't care—why should it hurt you? *(Intensely)* Then you do care, Anna! You do care!

ANNA *(Struggling—feebly)* No. I didn't mean—

ANDERSEN *(Triumphantly)* You do love me, Anna! You do! I told you last night I knew you must—must!

ANNA *(Trying to force her hand away from his)* No, Paul! No!

ANDERSEN *(His voice thrilling with joy)* You're lying, Anna. You know you are. You can't blot it out of your eyes. It's there—giving you the lie— *(He tries to press her to him. Chris again takes a step forward, crouching, his face convulsed with rage; but there is some fear which stays him, holds him motionless in his position of eavesdropper)*

ANNA *(Desperately)* No! *(Half-hysterically)* I—I don't— *(Then breaking down)* Yes—I don't know— Oh, what am I lying for this last night— Yes, I do—I think I do—I do love you, Paul. *(Chris shrinks back, seeming to crumple up as if he had been struck a mortal blow)*

ANDERSEN *(Drawing her to him fiercely)* Anna! *(He bends to kiss her)*

ANNA *(With real entreaty)* Don't kiss me! Please, Paul! I ask you—please!

ANDERSEN *(Releasing her—tenderly)* But why?—dear.

ANNA It will only make it harder for us. I've said I loved you—and I do—but—I can't do what you wish—I can't marry you—never!

ANDERSEN *(With fierce grief)* But why not, Anna—if you love me?

ANNA   I should never have told you that. Why did you force me? But it can't be—I can't—I won't—I'm—I'm afraid.

ANDERSEN   Afraid? Of what, Anna?

ANNA   Of everything. Of myself—of you.

ANDERSEN   Of me, Anna? Of me? For God's sake, why?

ANNA *(Wildly)*   Don't ask me! It's enough to know it's impossible for us. *(Brokenly)* It'll be all right, Paul, in the end. After a time—when we haven't seen each other—we'll forget.

ANDERSEN *(Wounded)*   Forget? You can say that—but I—

ANNA   You've loved other women before me. You've forgotten them.

ANDERSEN *(Frowning)*   Has someone been carrying silly tales to you? Your father, eh. Oh, Anna, be sensible! Those things are nothing. They have nothing to do with the me who loves you. They are dead things, just as the old me is dead. I've played the damn fool, I know, but can't you see the change my love for you has made in me? Can't you believe in the sincerity of that change, its lasting quality? Why, I never knew the real myself till I knew you, Anna! Before that I just drifted with the tide, and let things happen. It was all a game to play. How could I know you—your love—would come to me? I was a fool. I never dreamed anything so splendid could enter into a life like mine. But now—it *has* come! Oh, Anna, I've

never known real love till I knew you! I swear it!
Can't you believe me?

ANNA *(Faintly)* Yes, I believe you feel that way—now.
But—you'd never leave the sea—

ANDERSEN *(Wildly)* Yes, I will. I'll work on land. I'll do
anything you wish, Anna.

ANNA *(Sadly)* No. Don't you see I couldn't ask that?
Your life is here. You'd soon grow tired on land—and
then you'd leave me—and blame me—and hate me!

ANDERSEN Anna!

ANNA You would—in time. And I—I don't want to
settle down, either—not the way most people do. I've
known the sea now, too. *(Sorrowfully)* I think Father
is right, after all. The sea does put a curse on the men
who go down to it—and their women—the women
most of all.

ANDERSEN *(Roughly)* Your father is a superstitious old
ass! He blames the sea for his own weakness.

ANNA *(Shaking her head)* No. He knows it better than
you. He has seen for many years what it has done. The
women wait, he says—and it's true. They wait. And
the men sail over the world—and there are the other
women in every port—fresh faces—and the men forget
their home. And when they do return for a short while
between voyages they and their wives are strangers—
and if children are born, the father and child are strangers—as I and my father were—and are. When my
mother died—he was at sea. *(Breaking down)* No, no,

CHRIS CHRISTOPHERSEN

I'm afraid, Paul. I couldn't live that way—waiting for you—not knowing what you were doing, thinking you might be drowned, fearing that even if you were alive, you had forgotten me for the other woman. No, no, it's best to end it now—in the beginning. I can't let my life be tortured like that! I can't!

ANDERSEN   But your father is speaking of the old sailing-ship days. What he says might have been true then. It isn't any longer.

ANNA   But you've told me yourself this ship has no regular route—that it goes any place in the world where there are cargoes, and takes them any place. If I were in the States now—married to you—when would you be home to me? You don't know. It might be a year— two years.

ANDERSEN *(Taking her by the shoulders and shaking her gently —compellingly)*   Listen, Anna. I've found a way to beat your father's bogie stories. You won't have to settle down in a landman's way—to a house and lot. I wouldn't want you to. I wouldn't love you if you did. I love the you who is different from the rest of the pack— the girl with the sea in her eyes, and the love of it in her blood—the girl who loves and feels the things I love and feel! *(Then buoyantly as if the vision of it were clear before his eyes)* We'll not leave the sea, you and I. We'll keep it in spite of everything. And we'll go to all the ports of the world and see them all—together! And the sea shall be our mother, and the mother of our children. And you won't have to wait for me as your mother waited for him —watching and hoping and despairing. No, you will be with me, beside me, a part of me—always!

ANNA *(Who has been leaning toward him, drinking in his words with shining eyes)* Oh, if that could only be! *(Then with a despairing laugh)* But it's only a dream you're dreaming, Paul. How is it possible?

ANDERSEN It is—when I'm a captain, Anna. A captain can have his wife to live on board with him if he gets the right ship and insists upon it. *(Resolutely)* And I'll win to a master's certificate just as soon as it's humanly possible.

ANNA *(Staring at him)* You? A captain? But you don't want that, Paul, you know you don't. You remember what you told me that very first night—the responsibilities you hated so.

ANDERSEN *(With a gentle smile)* And that is the biggest thing you've been afraid of—that I might be at heart a waster, after all—isn't it? *(She nods. He pats her shoulder reassuringly)* Well, you needn't be any more. Didn't I say I had changed? *(With joyous strength)* No, I want responsibilities now—loads of them—to prove to you I can be strong. *(With virile confidence)* And I'll win, Anna! I know I can!

ANNA Oh, Paul, I know you can, too—if you want to enough.

PAUL I'll show you! But you won't mind waiting a little at first—till I win to my own ship? I'll make it easy, Anna! I'll get a berth on some passenger steamer with a regular route out of New York, and you can live there and I'll be with you a lot of the time. And we'll save the money, and every now and then you can take a trip on the ship as a passenger. That won't be so hard for you, will it, Anna?

ANNA   No, dear.

ANDERSEN   And it won't be for long. I'll work my damdest, I promise you.

ANNA *(Suddenly looking at him with a provoking smile)* You seem to be taking a lot for granted. I haven't said I'd marry you yet.

ANDERSEN *(Smiling down at her)*   Oh, yes, you did! I heard you! You said you'd marry me tomorrow—in Buenos Aires.

ANNA   Oh, no!

ANDERSEN   Oh, yes!

ANNA *(With a happy laugh)*   Well—let me see—perhaps I did. *(He puts his arms around her. She lifts her lips to his and they kiss and remain clasped in each other's arms. Chris, since he had overheard the declaration of love made by his daughter, has stood motionlessly, the hand with the knife hanging limply by his side, his eyes staring dully out to sea, his whole body seeming to sag and shrink beneath the burden of loss he feels. Now that they are no longer speaking, the silence arouses him. He sticks his head cautiously around the corner of the cabin. He sees them clearly in the moonlight)*

ANNA *(Her voice thrilling with love)*   I was so sad, Paul— I wanted to be dead—and now I'm so, so happy!

ANDERSEN Dear! *(He kisses her again. The knife drops from Chris' hand with a clatter. At the same moment he stumbles blindly around the cabin toward them. The two break from their embrace and, seeing Chris, stand for a second paralyzed with astonishment)*

CHRIS *(With a hoarse cry like a sob)* Anna!

ANNA *(Instinctively stepping forward to protect Andersen— frightenedly)* Father!

ANDERSEN *(Savagely)* Damn! *(His fists clench but he does not move, his eyes watching for some indication of Chris' purpose)*

CHRIS *(Stopping short in a dazed manner—incoherently)* Ay vas coming for'ard from poop. *(He pauses stupidly)* It ain't no good—for fight—her. *(He nods out at the moonlit water with a slow motion of his head)* It's so! *(His chin sinks on his chest. His shoulders heave as if he were stifling a sob)*

ANNA *(Going and putting her arm about him—compassionately)* Father! What is it? *(Then, after a pause, as he makes no reply)* I'm going to marry Mr. Andersen tomorrow, Father.

CHRIS *(Nodding)* Ay know. Ay hear all you say from first.

ANDERSEN *(Indignantly)* You were listening—hiding around the corner of the cabin there?

CHRIS Yes—sir.

ANDERSEN *(Angrily)* Well, I'll be damned!

ANNA *(Pleading for her father)* Paul!

CHRIS *(Defiantly)* Ay gat right for listen, Ay tank. Anna vas only body Ay gat in vorld. Ay don't know you. *(After a pause during which he struggles to collect his thoughts, to reconcile them)* Yes, Ay hear all you say, sir —all Anna say. Ay don't vant for Anna love fallar go to sea, sir—no, py yingo, Ay don't!

ANDERSEN *(Roughly)* Nonsense, man! If you heard all I said—

CHRIS *(Interrupting him)* Ay know. You say Anna live on board with you—some time—ven you're captain. She don't vait—like her mo'der. Dat's fine tang, too. And you're smart sailor for make captain, Ay know. Ay vatch you on voyage. *(His voice commences to tremble slightly)* And Anna say she love you. Ay hear. And, maybe—dat's good tang too—for young gel like her. Ay'm too ole fallar for keep young gel. Ay'm ole fool, too, Ay tank. So—Anna—you marry him. It's all right —yes—Ay tank it must be—it's all right.

ANNA *(Joyfully—throwing her arms around his neck and kissing him)* Father! *(Andersen comes forward and takes Chris' limp hand and clasps it silently)*

CHRIS *(To Andersen—with slow resentment)* You say wrong tang, sir, Ay hear. Ay don't svallow anchor, no, py yingo! Ay ain't scared. Ay'm ole fallar, but Ay bet you Ay fight dat ole davil, sea, till last end come, py yimminy! *(He shakes his fist defiantly at the horizon. The captain's voice is heard from inside calling: "Andersen")*

ANDERSEN *(Raising his hand for the others to be silent)* Ssshh!

ANNA *(Confusedly—in a flurried whisper)* He might come out, Paul. Let's hide from him. Good night, Father. *(She kisses him and darts on tip-toe around the cabin to the right. Andersen follows on her heels, bending low to be out of range of the light from the portholes. Chris remains standing in a daze, blinking in the moonlight. Then he turns to go to the ladder to the main deck, left. His foot kicks the knife which he picks up. He holds it in his hand for a second, standing at the top of the ladder, staring at it dully. He mutters:)* Ay'm ole damn fool fallar. *(He flings the knife over the side disgustedly)* You take him. He's your dirty trick, ole davil! *(The door on the left of cabin is opened and Captain Jessup comes out)*

CAPTAIN JESSUP *(Sees the figure standing there)* Andersen? *(Then startled)* Eh? Who's that?

CHRIS *(Dully)* It's Chris, sir.

CAPTAIN JESSUP *(Angrily)* Eh? Chris? Oh. What the devil are you doing here, eh?

CHRIS Ay vas speaking with Anna, sir.

CAPTAIN JESSUP Oh. *(Then in a more friendly tone)* Your daughter's gone in?

CHRIS Yes, sir.

CAPTAIN JESSUP Better get forward where you belong, then. *(Then as Chris turns to go—as if he suddenly remembered something)* Oh—one moment, Christophersen.

Now that you're here, I've something to ask you. The bo'sun is done up with rheumatism, you know that, eh? Pretty serious. Goes ashore to the hospital in the morning. Not a chance of his being fit again in time to go on with us. Hmmph. Mr. Hall reports very favorably on you, Christophersen. He suggests that you—you've had enough of barges, I'll wager—well?—eh?—do you want the berth?

CHRIS *(In a stupefied voice)*   You vant me—for my ole job —bo'sun, sir?

CAPTAIN JESSUP *(Testily)*   Eh? Have you lost your wits? Didn't I make it plain to you? Do you want the job— yes or no?

CHRIS *(Looks all around him wildly as if he wanted to run and hide—then in a panic-stricken voice)*   Yes, sir. Ay take yob.

CAPTAIN JESSUP *(With a grunt of satisfaction)*   Good enough. *(He goes to the door—then turns with a smile)* Good night, bo'sun.

CHRIS *(Automatically)*   Good night, sir. *(The captain goes in, shutting the door behind him. Chris stands looking out over the water. As he does so a change gradually comes over his face. It softens, and a grin of admiration and affection which he vainly tries to subdue, forces itself on his face. He shakes his fist again at the far horizon, and growls in a sheepish voice)* Dat's your best dirty trick, ole davil! Eh, vell, you gat me beat for sure dis time. Ay'm ole fool for fight with you. No man dat live going beat you, py yingo! *(He nods appreciatively and turns to the ladder, unconsciously beginning to sing carelessly in a low voice as he clambers slowly down:)* "My Yosephine, come board de ship. Long time Ay vait for you. De moon, she shi-i-i-ine. She looka yust like you. Tchee-tchee. Tchee-tchee. Tchee-tchee. Tchee-tchee." *(He saunters slowly front toward the forecastle along the main deck grumbling cheerfully as he does so:)* It's hard yob, bo'sun on dis rusty tea-kettle—yust vork, vork, vork all time. Ay better turn in for sleep, yes.

as

(The Curtain Falls)

About the Author

EUGENE O'NEILL (1888–1953) is one of the foremost American dramatists of the twentieth century. He wrote his first play at age twenty-four, his early experiences as a prospector and sailor and later as a reporter providing him with ample material for his career as a writer for the stage. His major works include: *The Emperor Jones* (1921); *The Hairy Ape* (1922); *Desire Under the Elms* (1925); *The Great God Brown* (1926); *Strange Interlude* (1927, 1928); *Mourning Becomes Electra* (1931); *Ah, Wilderness!* (1933); *Days Without End* (1934); *The Iceman Cometh* (1946); *A Moon for the Misbegotten* (1952); and the posthumous works *Long Day's Journey Into Night* (1956), *A Tough of the Poet* (1957), and *Hughie* (1959). Virtually all of O'Neill's Work is published by Random House.

Leslic Eric Comens is a lawyer in the New York law firm of Cadwalader, Wickersham and Taft, which represents Yale University's interest in the O'Neill literary properties.